My JFDI Way to Creating Credibility

Ian Houghton

www.CreatingCredibility.com

My JFDI Way To Creating Credibility

This is a work of non-fiction. This publication is designed to provide accurate information on the subject matter covered. It is sold on the understanding that the publisher is not engaged in rendering professional services or advice. The information is not intended to replace any legal council or other professional directives. If the professional services or advice or other assistance is required, the services of a professional should be sought.

ISBN: 978-0-9863263-2-5

Library of Congress Control: On File With The Publisher

Published by JFDI Publishings
        www.JFDIPublishings.com

This Book may be ordered by visiting www.JFDIPublishings.com

Printed In The United States of America

Dedication

Arthur Paxton
(January 1930 – September 2013)

I want to dedicate this book to my Grandpa who sadly passed away while I was writing it. My Grandpa had a profound impact on my life and we both shared many, many fun times in 'Grandpa's room' together playing with tools and electronics, taking them apart and putting them back together again. My Grandpa was an incredible person, so highly knowledgeable about so many things and respected amongst his peers. *He said what he liked and he liked what he bloody well said.* He had an *incredible* sense of humor and was always quick of the cuff with his responses. I'll forever cherish the moments we shared together and I miss you very, very much and think about you *all* the time. Oh, and I'm still waiting for my go-cart I was promised you would build me as a kid :0)

I miss you and love you Grandpa x

Acknowledgement

I would like to acknowledge first my students and everyone that has seen me on stage. This book came about because I constantly see how difficult people's journeys still are. It is because of you that I wrote this book. I, of all people, know how difficult it can be so I wanted you to know that this all came about because of you.

I want to thank Forbes Riley for not only being an incredible friend and woman, but also taking her own valuable time to write this incredible foreword for me and also being an honest genuine and sincere amazing woman!

I want to thank my family and friends that continue to support me as I continue along my journey. I know I can be a little hard work at times so I thank you all for putting up with me. Specifically Nik Halik who constantly keeps inspiring me to be better and better, Jeff Vacek who's just a genuinely great mate and genuinely cares about me and my future, and I really look forward to our future success together. I also want to thank Morgan Jones, another one of my best friends who is always there for me, we have such a great time together always laughing and joking around, you help to keep me sane at times and I genuinely appreciate our friendship.

I also want to express my gratitude for all the amazing 'stuff' that continues to happen in my life brought about by the universe and all the good things I do for others. It's appreciated and never ever taken for granted. I want to thank all of my failures, as strange as that may sound, for turning me into the person I now am and how you humbled me up too (although, no more, pls).

More than anything else, I want to express my all around gratitude and appreciation for everything. I don't take anything or anyone for granted; I'm always incredibly appreciative of all the positive things that head my way. Keep coming, I'm waiting for you with open arms!

Foreword

Growing up on Long Island in a middle class neighborhood I was always someone who dreamed of "more!" My dad, a printing press engine by day and an amateur magician by night, always taught me to find the "magic" in everyday life and the importance of being able to "amaze" people. Only problem was I grew up with frizzy hair, overweight, wearing braces for 8 years and had my nose broken when I was young by getting hit in the face with a baseball bat. I was smart, as book worms go, but painfully shy, not very attractive and quite the loner. At times, all I had were my dreams. I spent countless hours watching TV and sitting in movies theatres visiting exotic places around the world, wearing glamorous clothes and having untold adventures – but alas, they were all dreams – or were they? The Law of Attraction, what you think about, you bring about! Today I have visited exotic places from China to Africa, have appeared on the red carpet wearing designer clothes, starred in feature films and TV, even appeared as an actress on Broadway and have volumes of adventures from safaris to scuba diving, skiing the Alps to giving birth to twins! Has it all been easy – well who would I be kidding if I said yes – it's hardly ever easy, but always worth it!

One of my mottos, "You are the sum of the obstacles you overcome" speaks loudly to so many of us as bad things will happen but what separates the ones who succeed from those who fail, is not WHAT happens to you – but how you handle it, learn from it and grow from it.

One important factor in my change and growth from who I was, to who I am, was meeting fitness legend Jack Lalanne and his wife on the set of our Juicer infomercial in 2003 – I had just given birth to my boy/girls, feeling a bit sluggish and overweight but excited to begin this new chapter as mom. Jack, the "Godfather of Fitness" who at 70 years of age was so fit, he swam across the San Francisco Bay handcuffed and shackled pulling 70 boats had simple theories. "If man made it, don't eat it" and "cooking kills" plus he drank fresh veggie/fruit every day and never missed a workout. His genuine passion reignited something in me that has continued to propel me daily. Passion, commitment, and purpose.

He changed my life and changed the way I thought. I went from being a relatively unknown actress and TV host (even though I'd been on Fox's 24, ABC's The Practice and Picket Fences and hosted my own talk show on TCL and ESPN's X-Games) to becoming the woman I am today – a CEO, businessman woman, rainmaker, and motivational speaker. A highly successful and passionate trainer, businesswoman, wife, mother, author and actress. I created my own fitness brand of products including the SpinGym, a line of clothing, book and just launched the national talk show Forbes Living TV from the St Pete Production studios I built with my husband and partner of 23 years. Today I have sold over 2 billion dollars worth of products on live home shopping (HSN and QVC) and have appeared in the top grossing infomercials of all time. Funny how long it takes to become an overnight success. The secrets were clarity, focus, great mentors and a powerful, effective team.

I have personally known Ian for a number of years now and there is no question that what you are about to read in this book will change your life. Ian has been incredibly honest and raw throughout this entire book helping make your journey easier. If you follow what he tells you and embrace his system, you will make your journey easier and your life will become easier, no question about it (wish I had this book 10 years ago!) It wasn't until he systematically broke it down that I realized this was the same process that I went through just at different intervals in life and mine has taken the better part of my life – don't waste time – its too precious! I've witness Ian on stage speaking and even working with small groups - he genuinely comes from a place of love and compassion and a joy that comes from helping others. I've met his mom (a bundle of English energy and all smiles – in his case the apple does not fall far from the tree) and he's a lot of fun too! :0)

Success in today's day and age is based on trust, credibility and expertise. There is no question that you are making your life more difficult for yourself if you are not an established, credible individual. AND it's easier than you can imagine.

When I chose to "own my space" and build on the talents and success I already had, but in a systematic way I discover everything just got easier. I can meetings with people I admire, appear on TV talk shows and I'm constantly in the media and even managed to create my own TV show. Beyond that I get to enjoy traveling the world, speaking on stages and positively impacting people's lives through my books, seminars and online presence. I view the world differently now and know that my message is important. What are YOU meant to be doing with your time here?

Time is ticking away and you have no more of it to lose - so as Ian says, "It's time to JFDI!"

Good Luck and God Bless!

Forbes Riley

TV Host, Author, Health & Fitness Innovator, Founder of SpinGym, Keynote Speaker & Mom!

Table of Contents

INTRODUCTION

The point of this book is to tell the story of what I learned along the way on my journey of life and success and share with you what I discovered. For many years I couldn't get to where I wanted to be in life, until one day it hit me. Although I was hugely knowledgeable in specific areas of life and business no one would listen to me or pay attention to what I had studied my entire life, business, success and human psychology. Why did some people listen to some people but they didn't listen to others...? And then it hit me like a ton of bricks! OMG most people out there are not 'Credible' and that's why they have difficulties in life!

What people are not aware of, is that by not being credible it seriously affects their career and the speed in which they move forward and grow in success, business, career, relationships or

13

whatever it maybe. I am sure that at some point in your life there have been 'things' that you wanted to do in your career but haven't, or haven't been able to do, and the majority of time, other than possible ability, the reason for it is purely the lack of your credibility.

When you become known as someone who is highly credible I guarantee you, without a shadow of doubt they will take you more seriously, period! I tell you now, there have been many times in the earlier stages of my life in business where I wanted to do things and I couldn't because people wouldn't take me seriously. This was because I wasn't credible; my ability was still the same, but the problem was that I wasn't credible. Therefore it was really tough to have anyone take me really seriously, and it was incredibly frustrating and I know you feel the exact same way too.

So, the point of this book is to point out how to actually create and highlight your own credibility strategically; because once you create credibility in your life and your business, you can go in any direction you want effortlessly. Life will become so much easier as you will now be seen as being a highly credible individual. This is information that I have learned over the past few years of my life and I have been utilizing to catapult my career to a whole new level. If you utilize what you are about to discover in this book, you will literally shave years off your learning curve; there is no question about it. I realized that there is a really simple technique and system to this and once it is understood and acted upon, you will actually

14

be able to create credibility that you can leverage to further your career in whatever direction that may be. Once you know what it is you need to create and highlight, you will see just how simple it is. It's all about being strategic.

In 2009, I was inducted into the International Investors Hall of Fame by Robert and Kim Kiyosaki the authors of the Number One *New York Times* Bestselling Book - *Rich Dad, Poor Dad*. I remember walking onto the stage, and as I received the award it was the most amazing feeling I'd ever experienced. That weekend, it was like being like a rockstar for the *entire* weekend. Everybody upon everybody wanted to speak to me; everybody wanted to know me, everybody wanted to hang around me, everybody wanted to take me to lunch, dinner, and buy me drinks. It really was one of the most, if not the most, humbling experience I'd ever had in my life. For the first time not only had I gone out there and taken the steps and the necessary actions to become really successful in real estate and my career, but now I was being recognized for that and it was an amazing feeling.

What was really funny was that I didn't even know I was winning an award; it wasn't really until a couple of days before that I knew, so it was a total shock. I didn't know there was an award ceremony, I didn't know it existed. So, to find out that I had not only won this award but that I was going to receive it from - in my opinion - 'The Guru' of real-estate investing was amazing. I realized *what* an amazing experience I had gone through – it really was an absolutely amazing experience to rethink about it now.

As time goes by - I suppose like anything in life - life gets in the way and you lose your focus, sometimes you are not sure which direction to take. But, over a number of years and through having different coaches and gurus in my life and learning different things from different individuals, I realized just what I needed to do and I created something that was very simple to understand.

That is what this book is all about, it's about showing you and highlighting for you just what needs to be done in order to create credibility and become 'someone'. It is really funny because so many people fail to see the level of credibility they already have in life. I failed to see it when I was inducted into the Hall of Fame for real estate; I failed to see the level of credibility that gave me because, at the end of the day, it was still me and I've always been me, if that makes sense. I have never been anyone else; so for me, it was a very strange feeling to know that I was credible in an area that maybe I wasn't giving myself enough credit for.

In this book, you are going discover what I call the foundation to creating your credibility, to furthering your career in any industry you're in. No matter who you are, wherever you are in the world and no matter what your age. Once you understand what needs to be done and the power of creating it, this will massively change the way you live your life. The other thing you'll notice is just how fast your life will move once you get the foundations in place.

What is so clever about this is that you will see throughout the book how you can tweak your content throughout the years, to continually compound upon your credibility.

This book is going to show you exactly what you need to do in order to create high credibility within your industry; whatever industry that may be. I have worked with clients all around the world and in many different industries; it doesn't matter what industry it is, the truth of the matter is, that this 'Creating Credibility system' works and it is powerful, and once you know how you utilize it correctly it will massively change your life in a very short period of time.

Throughout this book, at the end of each chapter, you will see that I have left a section for notes. Here is where I want you to start to take action and write any ideas and things that come to mind; it's all about JFDI – Just F***ing Do It! You want to get to a point when you close the book, that you only need to go to the notes section, and the majority of everything you need to do is already written down. So please make sure you utilize the notes sections, they really are put in this book to make things easier for you.

Who is this book for? It is for anyone that wants to further their career. It doesn't matter what industry you are in. The truth of the matter is that it works. It can be tweaked and you will see as you continue to read through the book just how simple all of this is, and yet how somebody can raise themselves to be highly credible once they understand exactly what needs to be done.

I say this many times; *business is just a game, life is a game; it really is about who is willing to go out there and play it hard.* There are rules, and if you know what the rules of the game are, you will make your journey so much easier. Don't forget to play the game hard through to the end. Most people do just a half-hearted attempt of playing this game, remember we don't walk onto a field or pitch and play for second place, we play to win.

Throughout this book you are going to learn some more rules to the game, some more tools for your tool bag, something you can add to your repertoire as an individual, as a business person, as an employee, or even as a singer or a real estate investor. Trust me, of all people who understands the importance of this when it comes to a real estate investor, it is me. As I have said previously - creating credibility works in every single industry, anywhere around the world for any individual, immaterial of age.

You will hear me relating throughout the book to areas in business and in real estate because these are the areas I work in. However, I will highlight certain areas where it also works in other industries, so you can see where the pattern is. Once it is understood and applied, this book will radically change your life and your perspective to becoming highly credible and successful.

Not only that, but you will also see just how highly credible you become; you will see that other people begin to look at you and view you so much differently, with so much more authority and respect. They will stand in front of you and be willing to listen to what you have to say. Not only that, but they'll also want to hear more from you.

Why? Because you've now gone from a no one to a someone. You go from being someone who is not credible to someone that is highly credible; this will change your life, if you do it properly, believe me!

There is no feeling like it than when you become highly credible. You get the meetings you've always wanted and with the people that can make your life changing decisions. When you stand in front of someone, you are now a confident individual knowing that you've perfected the area where the true depth of content and knowledge lies and you can talk about it confidently. People now introduce you as the authority and not as 'who the hell is this person'.

The tables now get turned and people are coming to you, to do business with *you* and not the other way around.

This is a powerful, powerful system if used correctly.

Notes:

How credible do you think you currently are?

How credible do you think you currently are in the eyes of everyone else?

What industries do you worked in?

What industries have you worked in?

What company do you worked for?

What companies have you worked for?

Where were you educated?

CHAPTER 1:

MOST PEOPLE ARE INVISIBLE

Do you know that about 99% of the people out there, *you* reading this right now included (and as harsh as these words are going to be, they are here to help you), are invisible. That makes it very difficult for people wanting to do business with you; for you wanting to get a higher position in your place of employment, for you wanting to raise finances to buy real estate, for you wanting to be taken seriously in a business, for you wanting to get face to face with the person who can possibly make *the* difference in your life.

No matter what it may be that you are wanting to achieve, if you're invisible you are making the process of somebody wanting to do business with you significantly more difficult. If you can get to a point where you're not invisible, not merely not invisible but you're positioned as being someone who is highly credible and strategically thought about, this will make a massive difference to people and how they will perceive you. Not only will they pay more attention to you, but doing business you want with them will now be significantly easier!

The problem is this: most people, when they build their brand, build it around their business. Let me give you a great example of what I am talking about: Go and grab a bunch of business cards from everyone you know, or every single time you're given a business card I want you to pay attention to something and you will see that I am 99.999% correct. You will see this almost a hundred percent of the time.

Everyone will hand you a business card that relates to their business. Now, I know you might be scratching your head saying "Well yes, it is a business card." The truth of the matter is this: you want to give somebody a business card based around *you*. You are the brand, not your business. Your business is just a vehicle that sells the things to generate the income that you need. People buy from you. If you are more credible than others, you'll get the business. Period…. end of story!

People create websites and every single website they build is built around their business. What is the first thing you do when you are about to potentially go into business with somebody or meet somebody or date somebody? There is a high chance that you're

24

likely to Google them. Why? You want to know if they are credible. Not only are they credible, what are people saying about them? What are their reviews like? Are they good reviews or are they bad reviews? And if they are credible, how credible are they showing? Are they just about showing, are they just about credible? Or are they showing strong and highly credible in many different areas. I'm not just talking about the internet here, but there are many different areas where someone can become highly credible.

Once you understand and utilize that, your life will change, there is no question about it. Understand that your brand is built around you. If you are a real estate investor or wanting to buy a business, people are going to research you. If they are going to research you, what information are they going to find? Ask yourself the question right now: if someone wanted to research you, do you show first of all:

1. Do you show anywhere or are you invisible?

2. If you do show, how does that affect your credibility?

Let me give you a great example of this. Some people will sometimes post crazy pictures on the internet, these are things that can really come back to haunt you; you want to be really careful what you post. Now, am I saying that no pictures that will slip by? No, we live in a new era these days, and stuff just slips by, but you need to be careful about what you put out there because it will determine how people perceive you. How people perceive you is going to determine the level of credibility they give you. Understand, this *'perception is reality'*. So, think about how and where you want to be credible.

So many people don't understand this and so many people get it wrong, so many people come to me and say "How have you been able to catapult your career to the next level?" It was because I became consciously aware about highlighting the areas of credibility that I had built up in my life through my accomplishments. I knew that I knew the "stuff," the knowledge and application of my knowledge was never an issue. What became an issue was why somebody would want to buy from me over someone else? Why were they willing to pay my higher fees over someone else's lower fees? I realized it was based on my credibility.

The more I realized it was my credibility, the more I started to work on highlighting and creating this. The more I worked on my credibility, the more credible I became; the more credible I became, the faster my career moved, and the more money I made. It's about that momentum, building that momentum.

This is why successful people become more successful, it is because they are already credible. Does that make sense? Think about that for a second. Successful people become more successful because they become more and more credible. The ones that became really successful are the ones that were able to leverage that credibility to the next stage. Some of you may be sitting there now, and you think that you're credible. My question to you is: how credible are you really? If you and I were to be in contact or I met you in a restaurant one day and we were sitting chatting, and I decided to pull out my phone and research you right that second, what would show? Would it show good or would it show bad, or would you even show at all? That is the problem, it needs to happen now. No more time should be wasted; no more time needs to go by. Take action and JFDI!

I will tell you a great story. This only happened a few days ago, just before I started writing this book. In fact, it was last weekend. I live on the beach, I love living there, it is like paradise. I have lunch or dinner at the beach almost every day, why not, I live in paradise. So, I was sitting at the bar having my food and just watching the world go by, and I got talking to this businessman - smart guy. He sat down and we spoke, and I asked him what he did. He started telling me and he sounded highly credible. I thought he sounded great. He walked off to the bathroom and as he did I pulled out my phone and decided to research him quickly online to see just how credible he was. The truth of the matter was, not one single thing came up about him, and immediately he went from credible to not credible. This means for me I would not do business with him.

He is making his life significantly more difficult for himself because he isn't showing as credible even though he was credible. So when he came back and sat down I explained this to him, and he absolutely agreed with every single thing I said. He said, "You are absolutely right, I really need to build on my credibility." I told him that I could show him how to do it, it is simple. "Here's my number, give me a call."

Granted, it was only a week ago, so the phone may still ring, but as yet I still have to hear from him. I'm someone he sat next to, who is a leading authority in creating credibility - personal branding, who is highly credible myself, and yet he fails to take action he doesn't JFDI. Let me tell you something; you can learn about this amazing stuff that I am going to show you in this book. Remember, action is power, not knowledge. Knowledge is not power. Action is Power. Don't become one of those people who always talk and never do anything. Stop talking and JFDI.

When I first moved to America, I was 27 years old, and when I lived back in the UK working in my family's business. I was highly credible because of the family name. We had a very credible business. So when I came to America I wanted to get started in a bunch of different businesses that I was interested in. Moving here, I really wanted to give life a real go, but I kept stumbling into all these road blocks. No one would take me seriously, and it frustrated the hell out of me for years. I battled with this and I battled with that, I started this business and failed on that, started something else and I did it alright, but no one would take me seriously. I couldn't get the so called 'breaks' that I was looking for, and this was especially true when I got into real estate; this was where I noticed it the most.

When I was out there looking to borrow money from people to help invest and create win-win situations, it was very difficult, almost impossible. I wanted to buy properties and I wanted to get money to invest, but I couldn't because no one took me seriously. It was very difficult. Actually, the way I did it was I leveraged the credibility of my family's business back in the UK, for those of you who wanted to know how I got the deal.

Sometimes we just need to do things that move us to the next level; I did that and I wasn't really aware of what I was doing. That was a very subconscious decision I made at that point telling them about my families business, but I said to myself "Look, I know I can do this, this is my family, this is where I come from, and this is the business that we have, so now give me a break." And they gave me a break. Before I said those words, it was incredibly difficult. The reason was because I was invisible; I wasn't credible, nobody took me seriously and it sucked, and it made my professional career difficult and more than anything else it took so much longer than it needed to take. You may think that you are credible in your field right now, and you may very well be, but my question to you is this: on what scale are you credible?

Some people think they are highly credible when they have a high presence or high credibility in their city, but they don't leverage that to move their careers to the next level. Some people are only credible locally; maybe just in a town, maybe some people are only credible within their own family. But you can still be the same person and yet be highly credible. Are you credible nationally? Are you credible globally? Because when you are, your life and career will move to the next level. You are still the same person, it is still the same information, but now you are creating credibility on such a grandiose scale.

When you create this credibility, it can be in any industry you want, it can have any message you want it to have. Maybe you are a student wanting to get into a different college or university or a higher university, maybe you are looking for the "edge." Maybe you're a shopkeeper who wants to open more stores; maybe you're a real estate investor who is looking to move to the next level. Maybe you are a lawyer who wants to expand your practice and you want to be taken more seriously in your social circles because, if there's one thing this will do, it will definitely increase your credibility within those circles, guaranteed!

When you increase your credibility in your social circles, your social circles will also begin to increase too. Does that make sense? Think about what I have said. Highly credible people want to mix with highly credible people; end of story. They just do. The caliber I have in my friends now has been built because of my credibility plus being able to maintain humility at all times. That is where the introduction was first made, because I was credible, and then I create amazing friendship with some amazing individuals.

My social circles grew purely because of the introduction of my credibility. I also just happen to be a really nice person, and it is really important to be aware of that and also know that you can constantly tweak the message, tweak how you want your credibility to be seen. The message you want people to see, read or hear about you can always be adjusted.

Notes:

Are you currently happy where you are in life?

Are you invisible?

Do you have a business card? If so what does it say on it?

If someone researched you right now what would they find about you online?

Do you show anywhere or are you invisible?

If you do show, how does that affect your credibility?

What credible 'stuff' have you done in you life?

34

CHAPTER 2:

THE IMPORTANCE OF CREDIBILITY

You can make yourself highly credible by leveraging the existing knowledge you already possess; you don't need to go out there and seek a bunch of 'new' knowledge to do this. You already possess the majority of knowledge you will need, and if you don't, contact me and I can easily show you where your knowledge is. You'll find that as your credibility grows and you start to move into your niche area of an industry or whatever it may be (and again, it can be tweaked) you'll see that as you become passionate about that niche you'll naturally want to continue to increase your knowledge. You'll want more education; you'll want to learn more so you can help better others, because that's what this is all about - bettering others. When we better others, we better ourselves.

Why am I writing this book? Because it will better you, it will help you. In return, what happens when I help you? It is a no brainer; at some point you are going to hopefully want to come and get more things from me - more than just a book. Does that make sense? I want to help you, and if I continually and constantly help you, you'll have absolutely no problem in handing money over to me on the condition that you continue to grow. The only time you'll have a problem with me is if I stop giving to you; if I stop helping you and you stop growing. Until that point you will always want to keep working and learning from me on the condition that I help move your career further forward, by shaving years off of your learning curve as others have done for me too.

It is exactly the same way with you. Whatever you want to do, you are doing it for some other person; because, in return, they will then repay you. I talk about this in my *Outstanding Customer Service book*. I have paid a lot of money to learn lots of things throughout my life, millions of dollars have been paid in learning and mistakes, getting a better education, becoming better educated all around; personally, financially, business wise - it is important to find that balance.

You need to make yourself highly visible, it is so important. We just spoke about the fact that 99.999% of people are invisible, *they* are already invisible so... all you need to do is create your credibility and you'll make yourself visible and credible, and not just that but highly visible and highly credible. Once you are visible, people will take much more notice of you. You'll see how amazing this is; how much faster your career will rocket forward. How you now can achieve the things that you have always wanted to achieve in life and how you always hit stumbling blocks before, you will now find them disappear.

You have got to understand that people are going to find it very difficult to take you seriously if you are not credible. I do not mean to say that you don't possess that same knowledge because, of course you do, but the question is: are you going to buy from someone that's credible or are you going to buy from someone that isn't credible?

Think about it this way; you have two vehicles sitting side by side, they both look very similar and they look to be the same high-end quality. They are both exactly the same price, they are almost identical, even the fixtures and fittings and the leather look similar, it even smells the same. One of them has no badge to it and the other vehicle is a Mercedes Benz. My question to you is: which one are you going to buy? Same cars, same colour, same price, virtually identical; one has a Mercedes badge, and the other doesn't. You are definitely going to buy the Mercedes because it is credible - end of story.

Think about it with anything in your life. There may be two burger places - one is a *McDonald's*, the other is *Joe's Burger*. They are

37

the same price and they look to offer similar products, which one are you going to buy from? Most likely, *McDonald's*, because it is credible and you know what you are going to get. When people go to the Apple Store to buy Apple products, other than the cool factor, why do people buy them? Because they are highly credible. What you need to work on is having that level of credibility and it's easier to do than you think!

My mentors and coaches in life have been highly credible individuals, the circle of friends that I am privileged to be in, are highly credible circles. When you are in highly credible circles, you are highly credible and you are mixing with highly credible people, and meet *other* highly credible people, you become even more highly credible. Sounds funny, right? But, it is true. It just continues to compound upon itself. If you are a 'no one', people just won't do business with you, and then you get stuck in a rut of just being in the masses and not achieving the things that you want in life.

I have worked with so many people that say to me "But I don't have the credibility." Then I sit with them, and in five minutes I can point out where they are highly credible and the exact direction I would lead them. It is the same with everyone; I can find credibility in anyone; it's easy when you know how and where to look.

You are going to see in this book the directions that you need to go in order to create your credibility. Create your brand because your brand is your credibility - no brand no credibility; simple as that. If you don't have your brand established and the foundation work in place, you are making it difficult for yourself. As I said before, nowadays people will Google you, and if you are not "Googable", you are a no one, it's as simple as that. If I type your name into Google and you don't come up, you are a no one - as tough as that sounds, it is true.

You may be sitting there and you may have all these levels of qualifications framed and put up all around your walls in your home or office. They are absolutely no good to you, if you do not highlight them strategically. All these highly credible things that you have done in life, successes you may have had in any industry, as an entrepreneur or real estate investor, if you don't highlight them, if you don't show them, if you don't place them specifically and strategically, you are a no one - sorry.

Notes:

What is your niche?

Do you require more education or do you already possess enough?

Just how visible are you?

Where does you credibility lay?

What qualifications do you possess and are they being highlighted strategically?

CHAPTER 3:

MOST PEOPLE ARE ALREADY HIGHLY CREDIBLE; THEY JUST DON'T KNOW IT OR KNOW HOW TO LEVERAGE IT!

I wasn't aware of my own credibility before I started this process, and this process wasn't something that I went out there and said to myself :Okay, I am going to go out there to create my credibility." It just happened throughout the years subconsciously. I was working on this project and that project, and they kept compounding on my credibility. I didn't realize it at that time, I just got on with it and did it. I wanted to do this and I wanted to do that; as it turned out the things that I wanted to do just so happened to be the things that created my credibility. There would be so many people that would keep saying to me "Oh, Ian, you have written this book" or "You have accomplished so much in real estate, you know you are highly credible." And I would say "Yes, I know that, but don't people take me seriously and it's frustrating the hell out of me."

So, I would keep working on things here and there, and what was so strange was that the only person that wasn't taking me seriously was me. Everybody else was looking at me saying, "This individual is highly credible." I was the one really questioning myself because I just couldn't see it I'm sure if you think right now about yourself and the things you've done, there has to be a lot, think about the areas in your life. Look at the things you've accomplished, you are highly credible."

You've possess information inside of your head that can massively help and positively impact others, massively help their lives, help them do things that they want to do. The thing is, the world is so diverse nowadays that you can make money at anything; I don't care if it's walking dogs, I don't care if it is owning a business - the world we live in today allows us to make money anywhere from virtually anything. It is a lot easier to make a living once you are highly credible. It is so much easier to get help when you have a mentor showing you the exact things you need to get done and the order to do them in, which is why so many of my clients realize the power in this and have achieved so much success. It is incredibly important stuff.

All the clients that I've had in all the different industries they've worked in, and trust me I've had clients in every type of industry you can imagine, have dealt with every type of person you can think of: students, stay at home mums, business owners, entrepreneurs, employees, celebrities, athletes and so on. Most of these people just don't think they're highly credible, and it is not until we sit and talk that I am able to point out all of the areas that they *are* highly credible in. Even if it is just one area, we start on that area and we begin to build on that strategically.

We can look at all different areas throughout your life, if there's one thing we've done that is incredible. One piece of information we have, or a bunch of information, it doesn't matter. All of this information can be highly useful to others, we just need to position ourselves as credible to make sure that your information gets in front of them. In return, they will happily hand over their money to you; as you have to me in return for the cost of this book, and I will *always* over deliver for you.

You know, one of the reasons you bought this book is because you either researched me and found out that I am credible, or you have seen me speak and you have heard my message and know that I am credible or you looked me up online or you may even know me personally. Whatever the reason may be, something grabbed your attention and made you want to buy this book. You picked it up, read it, and decided there is some credibility to the points I have made in it.

Maybe this came from the fact that the front cover looked good, maybe not; I don't know, I haven't designed it yet. But, the truth of the matter is that you have this book and you're reading my words because I am a credible source of information, and we only need one small piece of information in the beginning for you to become the same. It is so simple; I have not come across one person yet who I have not been able to make this work for, not one!

The students that I have worked with who implemented these fundamentals have become even more successful and they are just amazed at how rapidly their career moves forward. Now getting the meetings with the correct people all the time is a piece of cake for them. They're closing deals now purely because they are thinking way more strategically about how they chose to place themselves to maximize their careers because now they are highly credible people.

Think about all the things you have done in your life, what information do you have that can massively help others? What is it? Think of the achievements you've made. Maybe there were things in school, maybe it was your recent promotion or a new position in work, an award, a piece of real estate that you closed on that made people take a step back and look at you differently. You became credible because you did the deal. Think about all the types of things you've done. The other thing is the more you add the more they begin to compound on each other, and the more credible you become. When you look at my website that compounds on the credibility I have. It was specifically designed that way; it was strategically designed that way by compounding on the credibility. Some of the achievements that I have had so far in my career are on that website for a reason: to highlight the areas of my credibility.

Maybe it's just that you are not aware of the accomplishments you already have; I come across this frequently. Many people are just not aware of what is going on around them and the accomplishments and things they've done. You're living in a state of subconscious awareness and not conscious awareness. You're not consciously paying attention to what is going on in your life, to the things you've done. The areas of knowledge that you possess, are areas you specialize in. It's ok if you did think this way, I did too. However now it's now time to change and become consciously aware of your accomplishments and strategically highlight them. Trust me you're about to explode to the next level.

When I was a kid, I used to be into car stereos. I know, it's sad, I apologize, it is what it is. Back then, I knew everything there was to know about car stereos, and I mean everything. I remember my father saying to me at the time "Ian, you major in minor things." So, I would know a lot of information in something that really wasn't really worth knowing about, and that was car stereos. The truth of the matter is I agreed with him back then, but now I view that differently. I knew what car stereo to buy, I knew what speakers would work with what, I knew how to install them, I knew which amplifiers to buy, and I knew what type of base boxes

47

were best. I knew it all. If anyone ever wanted to do something to their car stereo, they would come and ask me. Why? Because they knew that I knew my stuff. I was highly credible in that area at that time. I know, I look back on it now and I can't believe how much money I wasted on it, yet, it was just one more learning lesson.

Do you see what I mean? It doesn't matter how old you are, it doesn't matter what you do, whether it is car stereos or a business, you can still be credible in it. You just need to highlight the fact that you are, so people will start to pay attention to you and take you seriously. I'm not talking about the type of seriousness where your neighbors know you're "the man." I'm talking about the credibility that gets you in front of decision makers, life changing decision makers. Closing a two million dollar piece of real estate as your first real estate transaction as I did is a major piece of credibility.

Most of you are not highlighting the fact that you are credible. Think of the years that some people have put into their careers, into their industries, you cannot work those numbers of years and not possess a bunch of really important knowledge within that industry. Some people put in two years, five years, ten years, and some may put in over thirty years or even sixty plus! You cannot be in an area of business for a long period of time and not learn and understand *a lot* about it. In other words, you have to be very knowledgeable to have worked in a business for a number of years.

You will know all types of different tips, ethical tips, tricks, and shortcuts to making things easier for other people.

I recently worked with one of my clients who wanted to set up a self-defense class and she didn't know how to go about it, so she went through the "creating credibility program" and she thought that she was not credible anywhere.

I asked her what she meant and she said "I don't know where I could pull my credibility." I asked her what she had done and she said "I have worked in the police force for 25 years."

I said "Are you kidding me?"

She said "No."

I said to her that *that* was highly credible right there. "Police are credible, you have worked there for 25 years, you've saved people's lives while being a police officer – that's even more highly credible."

She said "Well, I also have black belts in different martial arts."

That is credible. So this is a person that wants to set up a self-defense class, is highly credible. She then also told me that she was a stunt double in the movies. Well, that is credibility right there. Then she told me about a month later (something she had failed to tell me at the initial meeting) that she was a bodyguard for a number of years. A bodyguard is highly credible, especially if you want to learn self-defense from someone. I would definitely want to learn self-defense from someone who has been in the police force for 25 years and that is used to dealing with maybe not the best people in the world. I would definitely want to learn self-defense from someone who is a black belt. I would definitely want to learn self-defense from someone who is a bodyguard. And I definitely would want to learn self-defense from someone who was a stunt double.

So I asked her the question: "Who were you a bodyguard for?"

She said, "Sean Connery and Keanu Reeves."

At that point I almost jumped through my phone on her as if to say, "Are you kidding me? This is highly credible stuff right now! These are very credible people and you can leverage their credibility to increase your credibility." It is called 'Branding by Association' and we will talk about that a little later. You may be setting up a self-defense class up right now and you may be reading this and saying to yourself, "Well, actually I am more credible than that person" and yet you are sitting there thinking that you are not credible. You probably did think that up until you read up to this point.

Make notes right now of things that are jumping through your mind "Oh, I am credible in this, I am credible in that, I have done this, I have done that, I have got years of experience here, and I have got depths of knowledge here. I am the only one that can do this, nobody does 'that' better than me, and I have come across something that no one else has come across." Start to list all the things that make you credible. The more you list, the more credible you become. The more credible you become, the more successful you become.

You need to leverage all of this information. You need to look at the things that you have done, the things that you are doing that are credible, and you need to leverage that to the next thing that is credible. These are the actions that will further your career that can help you put more money into your bank account. Now it is not about the money, but it is about the freedom, the opportunities that you can do with the money; the more people you can help, the more people you can contact and communicate with and make a difference to their lives. To help people is what it is all about, making a difference. When you raise your credibility and you are getting out there to pass your message on to someone else to help better their lives, it is an amazing feeling, trust me it's almost an irreplaceable feeling. You will find that you get results so much quicker, when you create your credibility.

Notes:

Do you view yourself as a credible individual?

What information are you very knowledgeable in?

Can this information help others?

Is it something you are passionate about?

List all the things you have accomplished in life, what are the highly credible things?

Do you have a passion that you are not making money on, if so what is it?

CHAPTER 4:

THE IMPORTANCE OF STRATEGIC THINKING AND STRATEGIC PLACEMENT

One of the biggest things I learned in my life was the term 'strategic'. I had heard it used so many times by so many people, but quite honestly I never really fully understood the true meaning of the word. Once I truly grasped the concept, it was without a shadow of a doubt, an absolute life changer!

The dictionary defines strategic as: 'Carefully designed plan to serve a particular purpose or advantage.'

The problem is; so many people don't think strategically. It goes back to comments I've made before, and that is that most people live their lives in a state of subconscious awareness rather than a state of conscious awareness.

What does that mean? It means that most people live their lives on autopilot. They wake up every morning, push the autopilot button, and do the same things every day without paying attention to them. This is what happens when you see or hear people say "this always goes wrong". You look at them and say "If it always goes wrong, then why don't you just pay attention to it, fix it, and make sure it doesn't go wrong again?" The reason they don't pay attention to it, is because they are living their life in a state of subconscious awareness - autopilot; they are not paying attention. The next minute 20 years or more have gone by and you're no further forward in your life.

Let me explain something; when you pay attention to what happens in your life, you can start to recognize what things are happening. What things are good and what things are bad, you can then do more of the good things and less of the bad. I know this concept sounds so shockingly simple yet 99.9% of people out there don't think this way. If you can learn to think strategically from this moment forward I guarantee you your life will change.

Every single thing that I do in my life is a strategic move. They say that your 'network equals your net worth,' and that 'you are the average of the five people you choose to spend your time with the most.' My question to you is this: is this a strategic move? Is your network equalling your net worth? If in your close circle of friends, or your close group of friends, you are the top dog in the group, you need to find a new group because they are holding you back. There's only one reason you want to stay top of your group and that's for the feeling of superiority and that way of thinking is already holding you back. I have known too many people that want to hold this role and let me tell you something about all of them, they are all absolute idiots and only seek self importance.

I remember as I grew up I always wanted to be the main person in my group because I thought it was cool - it had the cool factor, people wanted to listen to what I said because I was the top dog. As time and years went by, I realized that I had to shut up, and that it was less about me and more about them. The more I could build strategic relationships, the more successful I could become in my life. I know this might sound stupidly simple, but we are going to really cover this, in this section.

The importance of the word 'strategic', if you truly grasp its concept, will 100% change your life forever, and I don't make that comment lightly; I don't say it flippantly. I say it because it is true - if it works for me and my students/clients, it works for you. There are rules and laws of success, recognize what they are, implement them, and you will get the same results. If you throw a stone up in the air, it is going to come down. If you are standing in a tree and you throw a stone, it is going to head down; it is just the law of gravity.

There are laws that exist within the universe that, if we recognize what they are and we strategically play them to our benefit, we can't help but become more successful. I know you may be shaking your head now saying "I don't understand, this doesn't make sense to me, it can't be this simple." In this chapter, I am going to show you just how simple it is and if you truly grasp the concept, your life will change forever, there is no question about that! Excited…? You should be!

So, do you know that most people don't really know what the meaning of strategic is? Strategic, in my opinion, means how we choose to think about things and the way in which we think about them. The whole picture, looking at the end and working all the way back to current day and coming up with a solid plan to execute and how we make our actions, viewing all the fine subtleties. Let me give you an example that is the best way for me to explain this to you. As I am giving you these examples, I want you to start thinking about areas in your life where they may align with, where I may strike a chord that makes a lot of sense to you.

For years, as I was growing up as a kid, I would make friends; some of them I would keep, some of them I wouldn't, and some of them I would outgrow, in fact if the truth be known the majority of them. So, as I started to get deeper into my life and become more successful in business, I really started to look into the relationships

58

I had. I had finally created strategic relationships on autopilot and thankfully I was able to create them on autopilot because quite honestly I didn't have a clue what I was doing. Now I play this game hard. Yes it really is just a game and so is life so learn the rules and play it hard!

What do I mean by game? Let me explain; without a question, life and business are a game. There are rules. You play the game hard, you will win, no question about it. You go out there and you play the game with a half-hearted attempt, you will be given half-hearted results in return - there is no question about that either. This is your game, your life, your business, how hard do you want to play it? Do you play to win, do you play to just exist, or do you play for total domination? You now need to be very strategic in everything you do. When I had my friends, I would look at these people and I would say to myself, "Are these people that give to me? Do they give to Ian Houghton? Or do they take from Ian Houghton?"

Now, think back to times in your life when you had friends. There are friends that do nothing but cause drama all the time - that is all they do. Yet for some reason or other you keep them in your life. You may have kept them in your life because they were friends from high school or even earlier than that and maybe they are even family members. Let me tell you something; in this game of life, the game of business, I do not believe for one second that it takes fools lightly. Fools could be people that are not interested in the game of life, or fools could even be people like yourself who are just not taking any action and wondering why nothing ever changes. Why choose to allow other negative influences within your life and therefore continually suppress yourself? Which, FYI, is what happens. Okay, I know I might have gone a little bit deep there, but just trust me, go with it for the moment.

I looked at people in my life and I realized, I must get rid of some of these people. Now, let me tell you something; I of all people know how tough this is - I get it. I don't say this as a throwaway comment either, I say it, I understand and recognize the importance of it, and at times the difficulty of it. Here I am writing my second book right now, at thirty-five years of age. I say that it is difficult and that it is tough because one day I woke up and realized that the most negative influence, at that time in my life, was my wife. People who have heard me speak on stages around the world; have heard me talk about this. I am not saying for one second that we should go out there and divorce our partners. I am saying that we need to become consciously aware of the influences that are around and in our life, it's time to start thinking strategically, time to take action and time do something about it.

It was not for me to want to change who she was - she was happy with the individual she was, even though deep down she was utterly unhappy. She had to come to the decision on her own that her life was unhappy and that she needed to make changes. As it turned out, that wasn't the case. She seemed happy and content in her life and the decisions she made, and that is okay and I wish her all the best. However, those decisions weren't in alignment with me and my life, and the strategic moves that I made. I know I digressed for a second there, but I believe it is so important to understand.

So many people just don't get it; I made this move because I knew it was the correct thing to do for both of us. If you get it, then you can become consciously aware of it and fix it - so simple. So, as times go by, I would look at individuals I'd meet and I would say to myself "Is this a strategic alignment for a friendship for me? Are these people that can give to me emotionally, mentally, can they mentally stimulate me? Are they people that are more successful in a certain area than me?" They may be successful in marriage, successful in business, they may be successful in money, and they may be successful within their body as in being a physically fit human being. But, every person I align myself with now, is a very strategic move. Do I want myself to be aligned with these people, yes or no? If yes, then I give 100% of myself in return too and people who know me, know that to be true.

How do I come to the conclusion whether I want to be aligned with them? I look at the success they have within their life. Do they fill their life with drama? If they do, Ian Houghton isn't interested. Ian Houghton lives a life of true inner peace. Let me tell you something, when you shed all negativity and you live a life of true deep inner peace, your life will change. People cannot help but be drawn to the energy you have. I go out frequently, and every time I go out people are constantly drawn to me. Now, it is not always because of my accent (though sometimes), or the way I look, or the way I carry myself; it is because of the energy I have. It is because of the knowledge I possess and the confidence that comes with. People know that when they talk to me they are talking to someone who is smart, someone who cares and about others and someone who is able to maintain humility.

If you have heard me on stage speaking, you've heard me say that I am not academically educated; I left school when I was sixteen. One of my friends says I am a graduate of OCU (On the Corner University), I'm street smart. I am certainly not knocking anybody that is smart with their academics, but the whole point of this is about being strategic. All of the friends I have are very strategic friends.

I look at my life and I know that I possess a large depth of quality knowledge in a specific area. However, there are areas of my life that I don't possess certain amounts of knowledge. Let me give you a great example; I know a fair amount about the Internet and how to make money on it, but I don't know it all. For me to sit there and learn it all is tough; it takes a long time for me to figure it out, especially with the way the industry moves so rapidly. So, I chose to make a strategic friend within the Internet marketing industry. Someone that gets the game, that understands the industry. Now, if I need the best of the best information regarding online marketing or the Internet, I go to my friend and, do you think my friend charges me for his knowledge? No, because he's my friend.

Let me explain this, it is vitally important that a friendship be built before you turn it into a business. One of my best friends says to me 'drill deeper.' Get to a deeper level friendship; my friends know that I would take a bullet for them any day of the week, and I know they would do the same for me. Everyone in my life is a strategic partner; a strategic move I made to help better and further my life. My question to you is this: are you making those strategic moves?

So, I want you to think about what strategic means to you. There is a dictionary definition of the word; look at it, understand it, grasp the concept, and then play it hard. This is your life, you have got one shot. In fact, as I am writing this book right now; last week I lost my grandfather, it was a very painful time for me, and it was fairly unexpected. Here I am living in America doing every single thing I can do to catch a flight back to the UK to see my grandfather. Unfortunately, he passed on my way to the airport, and I will never be able to see him again. But, as I stood in his house looking at all the tools he had and how he made me as a person, I realized I wouldn't be where I am today if it wasn't for him. But, it makes me look at my life and wonder, am I doing enough and would he be proud of me?

The best that I can do in my life is to help, to give to you; this is a strategic move for me right here to lay my heart within this book. To give you everything I can, to build a relationship with you that, when you see me for the first time, you will come to me and know who Ian Houghton really is. I am not here to bullshit anybody, I am not here to rip anybody off or even take advantage of people, trust me I know plenty of people who are and nothing grinds on me more; I am here to help you become a better and more successful person.

You wouldn't believe just how much I've studied and money I've lost in life, to be able to teach you all I know. Every single thing I do in my life, whether it is good, whether it is bad, I'm always happy to give you information. To help others live a better, more fulfilling life; because, let me tell you something, when you live a life of true fulfillment you are going to have all the money in the world and nothing will ever compare to the feeling you have - it is an amazing feeling.

Knowing that I, Ian Houghton, come from this tiny town in North Wales called Conwy, how is somebody like me able to influence other people's lives for the better? I still scratch my head, even as I write this now, but let me tell you something; it is one of the most humbling experiences, at the age of thirty-five, when people come up and say that I've changed their lives, just because of the words that have come out of my mouth. I do what I do for you - to make your lives better, to make your journey easier. To shave years off your learning curve as others have done for me, this is one of my ways of giving back.

So again, it is all about being strategic; what message are you constantly putting out into the world? Is there a strategic message? Do you think about the things you say before you say them in front of the people you say them to? If you're saying things in front of people, are they strategic words? Have you really thought about them?

Have you ever heard somebody say something and the moment they say it, you say to yourself "What an idiot! I can't believe they just said that." They weren't thinking strategically at all. We have a phrase in the UK: "They open their mouth and let their belly rattle." It means they just opened their mouth and say whatever they wanted to say without thinking about it. Without choosing their words while making themselves look stupid.

People want to speak all the time, yet don't want to listen so much, and it is by the listening that we can make a true change in our life. Let me tell you something, success leaves clues; it is as simple as that. We just have to recognize what the clues are and make more of them happen. It's not about reinventing the wheel; it's about finding the correct wheel for the correct vehicle. *Success is not about one thing; it is about thousands of little things.* The more of these little things you do, they begin to compound on each other; the more they compound, the more credible you are, on the condition that you highlight them strategically - that is the whole point of this book. It is about raising your conscious awareness level in all of it. For you to become highly credible, you must start to think strategically every single day.

A few months ago I was speaking at an event and made a very strategic friendship with a very well known celebrity. Now, why did I build a relationship, why was this a strategic move for me? Very simple; because I knew that first of all, not only could I make a new friend, but the contacts that this friend had could make a massive difference in Ian Houghton's life and me in their life too, win win. So, the first thing I do is build a deep meaningful friendship. I would never do this with somebody I didn't like; I would never do it for their contacts. I do it for the people I genuinely care about. You know what it is like when you have friends, you want to help each other. So, let's be strategic and also make friends with people that can better our lives and we can better theirs; that is strategic thinking right there.

We all have friends possibly all over the world, maybe in our town, maybe our village, maybe in our city - and the majority of them are doing no good to you at all. It is nice to hang out with them – great, but be strategic in your thinking about that. Where does that friendship really take you? If it is a strategic drinking buddy then great, but recognize that it's nothing more than a strategic drinking buddy. If this is a friendship where two people can mutually benefit from the relationship then that is a strategic relationship that needs to be built on. If you don't build on these relationships, you are not playing the game hard enough - the game of life - you are not out there to win. Do you want to win or do you want to lose?

Let me tell you now, it is either black or white; you either win or lose. Winning for everyone is different; sometimes it can be based around money, sometimes it's material things, sometimes it can be based around love and a partner. The question to you is; are you thinking strategically? What do you want out of life? You really should go to the Notes Section of the book. Jot down in the book what is it that you want. Then it is up to you to go out there and JFDI!

I know you may say, "Well, it's okay for you to make these comments about all these places you can build strategic relationships." Yes, but the answer was in the comment there. You are in places that you can build strategic relationships.

My question to you is this: are you putting yourself in places where you can build strategic relationships? Does that make sense? Because I do, do you? When you talk to people, what are you saying to them? Have you strategically thought about what wants to be said, or are you just "opening your mouth and letting your belly rattle"?

My friends love me for many reasons, but one of the main reason is that I am always giving to them; always giving to their lives, giving help and support, always coming up with new ideas to make money, to leverage existing relationships, to build new strategic relationships and for having a lot of fun. So, when you are standing talking to people, are the words coming out of your mouth strategic? What I mean by that is: are the words coming out of your mouth, words that are going to make a positive impact on the person that is listening to you? Are you going to make them say to themselves: "This is a smart person; this is somebody that I need to be around - somebody whom the longer I am around, the more I can learn from them and grow."

Now, let me tell you something, in my circle of friends I am toward the bottom of the totem pole. That may be based around income, whatever it is, but I would much rather be the bottom of the totem pole around my circle of friends because they love me and they are going to help me get to the next level. So, I will take it, I have multi-millionaires, billionaires as friends, and I am nowhere near that level yet, but there is no question that it will happen - it can't *not* happen. It has to happen; you can't continue to be around multi-millionaires and billionaires and not grow, if you don't, then you are an idiot. I keep it real and tell it like it is all the time, for the benefit of making other people's lives easier.

So, my question to you is the message that you put out there to the world, which may sit on your website, it may be on your business cards, it may be the words that come out of your mouth, are they strategic words that are going to position you in the best possible light? When you write a copy for your website - take a look at my website - the front page of my website is strategically worded, strategically designed to compound on the credibility that I have build up over the last few years. When people read that copy, it is to the point, it tells you who I am, it tells you what I do, and it tells you how I have helped people and the people I am aligned with - it is very strategic copy. What is your copy and is it strategic? If it isn't, it needs to be.

You need to be strategic in an area that you are passionate about. Let me explain what I mean; here I am writing this book right now and if you could see me you would say: "This guy is very passionate about what he does." I'm sure it even comes across in the book; a lot of people often say to me that they can even hear my accent in my book, my text messages, and my emails.

I am very passionate about what I do, therefore everything I do in my life is based around the passion that I posses within that field, within that industry. If I was passionate about car stereos, which I was very passionate about as a teenager, then I would be an idiot to go into an area of business that was not based around car stereos. Yet, what is so funny is that so many people run their business, live their lives, make their money in a field or industry that they are not even the slightest bit passionate about. When you 'try' to earn a living in an area that you are not passionate about, you are not going to make much money. I am just telling you straight out right now, you just won't. Even if you are making a million dollars or ten million dollars a year right now, you are losing a fortune elsewhere, because you are not living your passion.

I am very strategic about the things I do; this is a strategic book for me to write, for me to get my message to you, for you to realize that creating credibility is a very strategic and powerful move for your career; there is absolutely no question about it. By the end of this book you will be thinking differently, you will be thinking in a very strategic way, a way that is going to create your credibility and compound on that credibility you already possess, therefore separating you from everybody else and making your life easier. Everyone out there is invisible; no one wants to do business with someone that's a nobody. If you are highly credible and your credibility compounds, your life, your business, will be guaranteed to become easier - I am living proof of this.

People buy from you because you are passionate about your industry. People get drawn in when I speak, when I talk, when I help them with their business, with their personal life. They get drawn in because they see the passion that I have in this area - I love to help. There is no greater feeling in the world to know that I make my money from helping others, which is what I do, and it is the most humbling experience and yet the most rewarding. I can promise you, people will always buy from you when you are passionate about what you do.

The other thing about being passionate about what you do, is that you will always continue to educate yourself. People that have

70

seen me speak know that I have a slight frustration with doctors and lawyers. If you are a doctor or a lawyer and you are reading this right now, this is going to make a massive difference to your success; most doctors and lawyers don't give a damn about anyone but themselves. They come out of university with a certificate that gives them the right to practice law and medicine. I rephrase the word 'practice'. A GP (general practitioner), he practices medicine. Some of them continue to educate themselves, but they educate themselves within their field rather than an education within a way to make patients or clients lives better.

This is why my whole ethos is about the customer; customer service, customer experience. What experience do you usually get with a lawyer? Is it a positive experience or a negative experience? I'm pretty sure you already know the answer to that question, so I don't even need to answer it for you. I think the simple fact that we see customers move from one lawyer to the next, to the next - to the next - is a great example of poor service.

If you are a lawyer sitting reading this right now and this is not the way you run your practice, guess what, you're different, and I applaud you and commend you for that. When you are passionate in an area that you love, you are always educating yourself. I educate myself all the time, every day. I don't sit there reading books for hours or researching for hours; what I do is put in the time to learn, research, and read because it isn't work for me - I am learning about more stuff I love. The more I love it, the more I want of it - it is as simple as that because it's my hobby. More than that, it keeps you on top of your game, the top of your industry all the time because you are the one that has all the knowledge - because to you this is just a hobby. Your job isn't a job, your job is a hobby and when your job becomes your hobby you just can't get enough; you want more and more and more - and why shouldn't you? All the information that we need out there pretty much is free - we just have to go and get it.

When I came out of my divorce, which was brutal; I had been kicked in the gut, I had pretty much lost all of the hard work that I put in over the previous years. It was gut wrenching, heart breaking; I felt like the biggest idiot and loser that has ever walked this planet. All the real estate that I'd built up, all the massive passive income that I'd built up – the majority of it was pretty much gone in a short period of time. I felt like I wanted to be like an ostrich and just bury my head in the sand indefinitely. I felt so embarrassed to even show my face, it was a brutal time in my life for me and I was really unsure if I would ever come out of it.

I remember it was at that time I wrote my first book. It was so funny because here I am, a few years later now, and I look back on it and I am not ashamed to tell my story anymore. A few years ago I was very ashamed to tell my story because I felt like a failure, but success leaves clues; people who are successful continue to be successful, immaterial of what happens in their life. Let me tell you something you NEVER learn when you succeed, you only learn when you fail and I wouldn't take advice from someone who hasn't failed, because they just don't know the patterns of failure.

Since my divorce, my success has skyrocketed beyond belief; for me it is incomprehensible. It is absolutely amazing what I have accomplished. Even though I still sit here writing this book, I still look at my life and say "Well, I have not really done anything yet," but it was pointed out to me, once my divorce was final, "Ian, look at what you had accomplished." This was pointed out to me by somebody I held in very high regard. For that person to recognize me, my accomplishments and credibility made a massive impact on who I am today.

It's the reason this book is being written for you - I am not writing this book for me because I know this stuff, I get it, I understand it, I do it everyday. I write this book to get the information out to you and you only. To help you have a better life, for you to become truly fulfilled as an individual, and if I have a hand in your life's true fulfillment then it is an incredibly humbling experience for me, but I will take it, because when you tell me that, when you come to me and shake my hand or you do whatever it is that you feel you need to do, you'll make my day and possibly bring a tear to my eye too (although that will be behind doors).

When I go home at night and I sit there and reflect on the day, I am so thankful for the people who have come to me and said that I have changed their life. Me, Ian Houghton from a tiny little town in North Wales. My credibility and my words had made an impact

73

on other people; it is an incredibly humbling feeling. It was pointed out to me, that the credibility I already have - even though I lost the majority of my real estate - the knowledge I have didn't go anywhere, it didn't move, it didn't change. In fact, if anything, it became even more powerful because I saw the areas where I made mistakes. Now when I teach real estate and help people become financially stable through real estate, I can give better service because of my mess-ups. That's how I learn. Now I align myself with individuals strategically to reduce the amount of mess-ups I make in my life. This book that you are reading word by word is designed to reduce the mess-ups you make in your life and massively reduce your learning curve too.

I knew my abilities, I knew what I could do, but I just didn't know if anybody would want to listen to what I had to say. It wasn't until I stood on stage for the first time and I was prepared for the speech. I had worked on my content for months; when I stood on stage for the first time and I had hundreds of people look at *me,* I could see that they were so totally wrapped up, engulfed in the knowledge that I was able to give to them - it was just an amazing feeling. My abilities were never in question; the only thing that was in question was the confidence within myself.

The whole point of this book was that I realized that once I created my credibility, and I was really strategically thinking about how I had created it, the change it would make in my life was huge. I went from a 'no one' to a 'someone', and when I became a someone everyone wanted to listen to me and do business with me. Everyone wanted me to speak at their events, everyone wanted my help, everyone wanted my advice and no one ever questioned my words or my knowledge. I was the same person I was before I had just highlighted my credibility. Understand what I have just said; *I was the same person as I was before, I possessed the same knowledge, the difference was I didn't highlight my credibility.* I put it in a place where it kept compounding upon itself to make me more and more highly credible. The question to you now is; are you strategically putting yourself in places that are going to create and compound and extend your credibility. Are you highlighting your previous accomplishments that are credible and are they getting you to the next level?

Every student and client I have, came to me and said that they were not credible and in less than two minutes of talking to them I find an area that they *are* highly credible in. Let me explain this; if you have been working in an industry for a number of years, you can't help but be highly credible. The problem is that you are not seeing the worth within your own knowledge, within your own content. Does that make sense? You are already highly credible, you are just not showcasing it correctly – that's all it is and you're not helping other peoples journey become easier.

The point of this book is to highlight ways that you can do it, so that you can finally become highly credible. When you are highly credible, people take you seriously, and when they take you seriously, they pay you serious money. When they pay you serious money, now you can live a life of true fulfillment and get out there and help others become more successful and happy; more successful in work, more successful in play, more successful in their marriage, and more successful with their children.

It is about finding a balance in all areas; people say to me, money is not everything. Oh yeah? Give me all your money, go live on the streets, and then tell me money is not everything. People that make flippant comments like that quite honestly piss me off, because they think they are making a comment to make themselves look good. "I don't care about the money; it is not about the money." I get it, it is not about the money; the money is a bi-product of you helping others to find their way of life easier - that is it.

Money just makes you more of who you are; if you are an asshole and you have a lot of money, now you're are a bigger asshole. If you are a genuinely loving caring person and you have a lot of money; you now have more money to love and care for other people on this amazing planet that we all get to share. Money just amplifies who you really are, it turns the volume up on you. Go to the notes section now, there should be some real 'aha' moments there for you. It is time for you to get your credibility, strategically thought out, placed, aligned and put out to the universe. When you do, the universe repays you back; it is the law of attraction - the strongest law there is. Utilize it, play the game hard and you will win. Go to the notes now, start making as many notes as you can, that have come to you through this chapter.

Notes:

Are you living your life in a state of conscious awareness or subconscious awareness?

Who are the 5 people you hang around the most and are they positive people?

Is your network equaling your net worth?

In your group of friends who is the top dog in the group?

Do you fully understand the word strategic?

Are you playing the game of life hard enough?

Who are the negative influences in your life?

Are the friends you currently have in your life a strategic
alignment?

What friends do you have that are knowledgeable in different areas
to you and what are they knowledgeable in?

What message are you putting out to the world?

Success is about how many things?

Are you friends contributing towards your life?

CHAPTER 5:

HOW TO BECOME CREDIBLE

Now we are going to get into the real important stuff, the gutsy stuff; the ways that we can become highly, highly credible. As I said, this approach is an approach that not only I have utilized in my personal life, so I know this works, but... I have utilized it with a number of students, and their credibility and their success have been massive. What works, just works period!

There are many ways to become highly credible. I am going to tell you my ways, the ways that work for me, the ways that took my income from nothing to where it is today. I was able to take my hourly fee from just $50 and literally explode it because people's perception of me had changed. The quality of my content only

81

continues to grow because I live within my passion - remember we discussed that in the previous chapter.

The first way to become highly credible is you absolutely MUST write a book! Why? Because authors are credible, authors are authorities, period! Before I wrote my first book, everyone kept telling me, "Ian, you need to write a book, you need to get your message out there; you need to tell your story." I would keep saying "Really, me? I've never even read a book never mind write a book. Who on earth is going to want to listen to what I have to say? Here is Ian from tiny Conwy in North Wales; who the hell is going to pay attention to what I have to say?" The truth of the matter was tens of thousands, hundreds of thousands of people, millions of people. My message resonates and it resonates because it is real, it has impact and more than anything else, it is really simple and makes a lot of sense.

If you want to become credible, the first thing you need to do is write a book. It is vitally important that you write your book in alignment with either what you do for a living or what you want to do for a living.

Let me give you a great example. I have had students come to me who have been in the process of writing a book and they have been yoga instructors holding classes, but their book was written about dogs or art or trees. It was not in alignment with what they did. It is a great feeling when you become an author, when the delivery of books arrives at your house and you say "Wow, I took that from head to hard copy book all on my own." It is quite an amazing feeling of accomplishment - I will tell you now, *but* make sure it is in alignment with what you want to do. If you are the CEO of a water company, you need to write your book on water or how to run a water company because when you are standing in front of people, and they are potential clients; you want to make sure that you give them a book that is in alignment with your industry and what you do. They'll think you're a rockstar even if they know more than you, because you have been able to achieve something they think is almost impossible. Trust me!

Look at my books; my first book was on 'Outstanding Customer Service' because that is what every single thing in this world is about. My second book is about 'Creating Credibility.' There will be other books on their way; there is no question about that. Once you understand the system for writing your book and creating it, you can write as many as you want and you can turn them around very quickly, simply and very cost effectively, once you know the tools. The technology is available; I have the technology to make your lives easier - it's very simple, but you must write your book in alignment with your industry. If your job is sales and you have sold for years and you know the way to sell, write your book on how to sell. That way, when you're standing in front of people and you give them your book, it is in sync with who you are and what you do it makes you credible.

Don't go out there to be a business consultant and write a book on dogs. I have seen people do it; it's stupid, they don't understand the fact that all of their hard work and effort is totally and utterly wasted. If you are going to do something that is labor intensive, it's your time, make sure you spend it on something that is going to be beneficial to you in your life. When you have made all the money you need so that you can be financially free, so you can look after your family and you have enough money should anything happen to you - then write any book you want.

However, at the moment, we are talking about creating credibility, so you have to highlight your area of credibility and the way that you do it is to write a book, become an author - very simple. Write a book in an area that you possess a large amount of knowledge. Why? Because the book is easy to write, you already possess the content inside of you. For me to write this book about creating credibility I get it, I understand it, I know the importance of creating credibility and I know how to do it because I did it, I created the whole thing. So, for me to write a book on it is just so easy.

Make sure that your book is 100% in alignment with you, your business, and the movement forward with your career. If you do, people will look at you differently, they will look at you as the authority because authoritative people are authors. If this makes sense and there are any ideas coming to mind right now, jump to the notes at the back of this chapter and write some notes on the type of books you could write; maybe in some areas that will massively increase your credibility. Your credibility increases, your life and your business get easier - it is as simple as that.

Understand this… people have a perception about you, change their perception of you and you'll change your outcome forever!

We spoke about just one area of creating credibility; the other thing you can do to become highly credible is making sure your online presence is high and is strategically designed to make you look highly credible. If you Google me, you'll see I am highly credible; is it by sheer chance that that has happened? Nope, it was strategically designed. If you are credible, if you are someone, you are on Google. If you are no one, you are not on Google - it is as simple as that. So, it is really important to make sure that you have a high online presence and that it is a strategically designed online presence. If it is not, and your wording isn't strategic and the placement of how you have set yourself up to be viewed by individuals online is not credible, you are only making it more difficult for yourself. The truth of the matter is, you can change it at the drop of a hat - it is so simple - we can change information very simply. So, it is very important that you really utilize the Internet and you become strategically highly credible, online.

The third area that is crucially important to compound your credibility is for you to become a speaker. If you are a speaker, you are an authority. If you are an author, you are an authority. If you have high online credibility and you are highly visible online, you are credible. If you have all three, you are now officially a rockstar and highly credible. Is this starting to sink in? It is a fact that they all compound together. One without a doubt makes you highly credible; the fact that all three compound upon each other just compounds on your credibility, it is vitally important.

If you are a physiotherapist, write your book about physiotherapy; make sure that your online presence separates you as the authority for physiotherapy and then make sure that you produce content that you can speak about at events - that will increase your credibility. The higher your credibility is, the more you can charge; the more you can charge, the more you can get out there and live the life that you want to live and make a difference.

It is also so important to make sure that you are branded. Look at my logos on both of my books, my website, everywhere you go; if I am speaking from my slides, I make sure my logo is there. Make sure you have a logo, make sure your logo is built around you and not your business. Now, if you have a business, also make sure that your business has a logo, this is basic branding.

This little paragraph I am about to say here is probably the biggest and most important thing in this entire book, so pay attention to this: *your brand, your credibility is you, not your business.* What do I mean by that? When people want to do business with me, they Google me, they research me, not my business. If Ian Houghton is highly credible, Ian Houghton gets the business - it is as simple as that. This works in any industry, whoever you are, whatever you do. If you separate yourself from the masses strategically and build something that compounds on your existing credibility, people will be bending over backwards to do business with you. I know this because I live it, I understand it.

It is also important to make sure that you brand by association. What does that mean? There is a reason I have multiple photos with celebrities. One reason is because some of them are my close personal friends, and the other reason is because I can leverage their credibility.

I brand by association, you are someone if you are with this person. The photo of me and Sir Richard Branson of *Virgin* - highly credible. You have to be someone to be near Sir Richard Branson - there is no question. You can't just walk up to him on the street because you won't find him there; you have to be at the right place at the right time or be invited. For me, I knew where he was going to be, I was actually invited to speak at the same event as him, and I made sure I created a relationship with him so I could get the photo and build a deeper relationship. The photo changed my life, why? Because I then went from a no one to a someone - people looked at me differently. "Wow, Ian is with Sir Richard Branson the founder of *Virgin* - a living legend." So, for me to be with him immediately separated me as credible and all I do is showcase it. I put it out there that these are the people I am with, why? Because I can brand by association. Not only that but when we were talking to each other during the day he even came out and said to me "you know what Ian, I travel all over the world and speak at all these events and damn there are some muppets around, I've never even heard of most of them and most of them have zero credibility." That hit me like a ton of bricks because it's exactly what I was thinking.

You can also leverage other peoples' branding. Let us say you have worked for McDonald's for twenty-five years, you are highly credible in McDonald's - there is no question about it. Whether we agree with McDonald's or not, whether we like the food or not, they are a highly credible brand and you can utilize their brand to raise your credibility. If you have worked in a bank for a number of years, you can leverage the bank's credibility. I worked at blah, blah, blah bank for X amount of years - leverage their credibility, their brand. Just before I had the photo with Sir Richard Branson we spoke about how difficult people make their life. He said to me "Ian what people don't realize is that they are making their lives more difficult by being a no one, why do you think I did all that crazy stuff in the beginning of Virgin. I wanted people talking about me, I wanted to show just how credible I was, and boy did it work!" Yes it did!

Who do you know that is highly credible? Can you leverage their credibility? Do you have any celebrity friends? Do you have friends that have celebrities as friends? If so, ask them to introduce you to them and get a photo. Leverage what is currently available to you to increase, raise and compound on your credibility. This especially needs to be established in the early days. I hope this is sinking in and beginning to make sense. Anything you can do, any person you can get in front of so you can get a photo with them – do it. If you have the opportunity to leverage their brand or branding yourself by association with them, you need to do it. Do what is necessary to put yourself in those places, make the phone calls, and make it happen. Or as I say, JFDI - stop messing around; stop wasting your time, and Just F***ing Do It!

You also really need to understand the real power of compounding; the more you can work, the more information you've got. If you are a one-time best-selling author, you are credible. If you are a hundred times bestselling author, you better believe people are going to perceive you differently. What are all the accomplishments you've done in your life that are highly credible and can be highly compounded on each other to make you look like a 'god' in your industry? Because really that is what we are after, we are after making you look like a 'god' because the moment you separate yourself from the industry, people will want to work with you over anyone else - there is no question about it.

When people or businesses want to work with you over anyone else, guess what, you can put your prices up. Why? Because you've now separated yourself by recognizing and highlighting strategically your areas of credibility, knowledge and expertise while compounding them all at the same time. All because their perception of you has changed life now becomes significantly easier.

Notes:

Is it time to write a book?

What book would you write?

Are you currently an authority within your industry?

Are you Googable?

Do you want to become a speaker?

Who do you know that is highly credible?

What is your brand?

Do you have a logo?

CHAPTER 6:

THE IMPORTANCE OF BECOMING AN AUTHOR

After I wrote my first book, I still viewed me as me, nothing had changed, or so I thought. The funny thing was that other people now viewed me very differently, their perception of me had radically changed. Here I am now however, one and a half years after writing my first book and when people hear that I am an author and I've written a book, it blows their minds. I have this funny thing I always say on stage; it is so ironic that I became an author when I had never even read a book in my life. I actually have, since I made that comment, but the point of what I am saying is, I was never an academic, I was never great in school. In schools all over the world, there is always a person that is great at sports and whichever sport you put him/her into they were always awesome at it. Well, that was me; put me in a classroom, I couldn't figure out a pen from a pencil. But people looked at me differently because I had accomplished something they couldn't, and they believed that writing a book was hard work and very expensive.

I am here to tell you it is absolutely not - it is simple and it is cheap and it's hands down one of the most powerful things you can do to explode your career.

Once you understand the technology involved to do it, you can churn a book out anytime you want, fairly inexpensively and you can churn it out very quickly; if you work diligently on it, anywhere between two to three months. Think about that, two to three months and you can have your own book in your hand, and if you work really hard you can possibly turn it around in a month. Some people take years to do this because they put too much emphasis on the whole process and never actually do it. Stop wasting your time thinking about it and JFDI. You're hurting yourself by not doing it!

It was amazing how people took me differently; now they viewed me as this authoritative figure just because I had written a book. I was and still am exactly the same person – significantly more knowledgeable yes, no question about it because I continually educate myself, but everyone now viewed me differently. People that may not even really know me come to my house and see a

94

book of mine and say "You've written a book?!" and I answer "Yes, I wrote a book." They then ask "How did it do?" and I say "Well, it was a bestseller." They're amazed at the fact that I'm a bestselling author. I have stood in front of some of the poorest and some of the wealthiest people on the planet and every single one of them is blown away by it.

If Ian Houghton can do it, believe me, you can do it - there is no question - I am not any better, I am not any worse, I just figured it out. *If you want strong high credibility it is an absolute must for you to become an author.* The point of your book is not about making money. Do you want the truth? You are not going to make a lot of money from having a book, just being honest. However, it is not about making money from the book, it's about compounding and creating your credibility so you can stand in front of any person in the world and give them a copy of your book on your topic. They will look at you differently; there is no question about it. They will listen to you differently, they will take you differently, and they will pay you differently because you clearly know what you are talking about because you are an author in that field, you are an authority. Anything that jumps to your mind right now, go straight to the notes section and start to write down some notes.

Your book is now your business card. I'm not saying you go out and buy bigger trousers with bigger pockets to carry around your book in, but let me tell you something; I have closed deals on airplanes travelling from one side of America to another just because my book sat on a table in front of me. It was a strategic move; I was sitting next to a guy who was reading a very detailed piece of business documentation, so I knew he was into business. What did I do? I got my book out of my bag, and put it on my table in front of me while I continued to work. I saw him glance a number of times at my book and me, because my picture was on the cover, (that was a strategic move), and then he asked me "Is that your book?" "Yes, it is." At the end of it, I gave him a signed copy and signed him up to a large figure for one on one coaching; purely because I had the book, it is my business card. $75k in the bank "cha ching" yes please! Does this make sense?

Some people tell you that they don't believe it is a good idea to put your image on the front of your book. I can tell you, there is no way in hell that I would have closed that deal on the airplane, and a number of deals after that, if my image was not on the front of my book. The picture is a strategic move to make sure that I get them to draw their attention to me. Every book that I write will have my image on it.

Do I enjoy looking at the photo of myself on my book? No, quite honestly, I find it a little bit embarrassing, but there are two Ian Houghtons out there. There is Ian Houghton the businessman and his job is to go out there and make the real Ian Houghton money so he can live the life he wants and create more of a positive impact on other peoples' lives for the better. That is why my image is on there and that is why I dominate the internet in my name. I

96

want people to know that when they deal with me they are dealing with someone that is highly credible - because I am, I know my stuff - there is no question about it, as do you!

Make sure that your brand, your logo etc are on your book. Everything needs to be tied together; your book, your business cards, your website, they all need to have the same look, same font, same logo - everything needs to be the same. You know what it is like when you drive past *McDonald's*, you know exactly how it is, you can see it from however many miles down the road - you know it is *McDonald's*. You need the same thing built around your brand. Get your logo created and put it on every single thing you do. This will make your life easier, your credibility more impactful, and you can charge significantly more now because now you're different, you have now separated yourself from the market, from your industry. Why? Well it's simple, no one now does what you do, they've not positioned themselves like you have. That now comes with a premium and in return you give them all you have and more! Read my customer service book for the best information on this!

Always make sure that you have your book with you. I keep some books in my car, my bag, at my office, at home - pretty much wherever I am so I can get a hold of it and give it to anyone any time I want or need to. It is so important that you do in the early days, because you never know when you are going to bump into someone. If you don't have a copy of your book on you, take their information and send it to them without charging them for it.

Don't worry about making money from the book, care about the fact that if there are a thousand or ten thousand or one million copies of your book or books out there, then they potentially can get into other people's hands, and these people one day could become your clients. If your books are sitting in a box in your house and you don't want to give them out because you don't want to lose money by doing that guess what...? That's exactly what's going to happen.

You can only become successful when your message gets out there. Remember this and highlight it in this book right now: *spoken words evaporate, written words leave an impression.* When you write a book, you leave an impression on the universe; then the universe will look after you on the condition you keep moving forward positively whilst helping others. It will take care of you and will bring you the business that you've been looking for, because you have accomplished something that most people can't and won't. You never ever know when you may need a copy of your book, so just make sure you always have one with you, at least in the early days.

The truth of the matter is that you can also self-publish. Self-publishing is a very simple process - we don't need to go to a publisher and get an advance and get in bookstores; that's not the point. The point is not to make the money from your book, but to create credibility that comes with being an author. This is your time to tell your story, your time to shine. You will see throughout my books I give you stories, examples, areas to help you understand how it has made my life easier, or how I have made other people's lives easier. We all have a story, tell it, and involve people within your life. They will love you for it.

In my first book, I talk about how, when I was a kid, we went to Thailand and I never wanted ice in my Coke. When I'd walk into the hotel they, would give me a glass of Coke with no ice. I went to speak at an event where they'd obviously read my book, and they gave me Coke with no ice in it. As it turns out, I like ice in my Coke now - funny how things change. The point of what I am saying is that people pay attention to what you tell them, so what do you want to tell them? Let them into your life, let them get to understand and know more about you. If there is one thing about me, it is that I am open; I keep it real. If you've got a question, ask me, and I will be honest with you and tell you the truth. If I don't have an answer, I am not going to bullshit you either, but instead I'll be honest and tell you that I don't know. Can't be more honest than that right?

Honesty is so important, especially in the business world. There are so many people out there who are trying to rip the next person off. Who do you want to be and where do you want to be placed? What can you give the world? Because, when you give, you get back – that's just the way it is; but don't give to get back, give because you genuinely want to give. The universe will 100% look after you - it has to. It looks after good people and I genuinely believe that, and I believe it based on the life I've led. Also, if you mess up, the universe will kick you hard in your backside. We all have to choose which direction we want to go in and how we want to do it. What stories do you have, that can impact other people's lives - make their lives easier, make their journey easier, make their process easier? What stories do you have to tell that can get your message or point across to other people so they understand it? When you write your book and you take ownership of that book, it is just the most amazing feeling you'll get; the feeling of accomplishment that, at the end of it - after just a short period of time - *You* are now an author.

So how important is becoming an author to your career? It's hands down the most powerful thing I have ever done in my career and it catapulted me to the level I always knew I was meant to be and so much more. *You absolutely must write your book, I've been incredibly honest with you in this book so far and I'm being incredibly honest with you now.* Get that book written and don't waste time, if you want or need coaching let me know there's always coaching available to get the book written and to get you to the next level.

Don't waste time JFDI!

Notes:

Have you ever wanted to write a book?

Why have you never done it?

If you knew writing a book was easy, cheap and not time consuming would you do it?

Why is it important to tie all your content together?

Do you have any great life stories to tell people about what you learnt, if so what are they?

CHAPTER 7:

THE IMPORTANCE OF HIGH ONLINE CREDIBILITY

Let me ask you a question. When you want to do business with someone, when you want to date someone, when you want to buy something, when you want any information on anything, what is the very first thing you do in the world we now live in? *You Google it.* If we are going to buy a camera, we Google it and research the camera to see if it is good or bad, or if there are better cameras. When we want to do business with someone, what do we do? We Google the business - does the business look good, show good (high online visibility and reviews) or does it not? Most of them, you will find, don't.

I think we would all agree that if you are a highly credible individual, you are on Google - there is no question about it, which means that the opposite also is true. If you are *not* on Google, you are not credible. So, what if we strategically thought about and built something that was designed to highlight the accomplishments we had already achieved, the ones that made us even more highly credible? What if we dominated as much on Google as we could to compound and build on the credibility that we already possess? If I want to work with someone, I Google them; what is said about them, how and where did they show? Let me give you a great example.

A few months ago I was invited to a big business event; I don't really remember how it came about. I had a phone call and they really wanted me to go to this event. I turned up at the event and they pretty much rolled the red carpet out for me. Why did they want to roll out the red carpet for me? They rolled it out for this reason: they Googled me, and what they saw blew their minds. They were not expecting this young person to be so highly credible, and in their eyes I was beyond highly credible, the most credible person they had come across. So, they looked after me like I was just the most amazing VIP business authority. Yes please I'll take that!

If you are going to buy something from somebody and you are going to network/do business with them, what do you normally give the person? A business card, right? Do you know that everybody who gives a business card does it the wrong way? Why? Because I am not buying *your* business, I am buying *you*. I don't have a business website, I have ianhoughton.com. Why? Because they buy me, you buy me; the business I have is what they are interested in, but if I can't sell them on Ian, then no matter how good my business is, they are not buying.

So many people create their businesses based around their business and not the individual. You go to the business website and it is all about the business and not about the individual. In fact, usually if you can't find anything about the individual there may be a tab called "About Us" or "About Me" and it might give you a tiny little rundown on the individual. It is probably worded in a way that will make you want to shoot yourself in the head at the end of it because it is so boring.

The truth of the matter is this; what message do you want people to read about you? If you are going to hand them a business card, make sure it sends them to your personal website. That is where you highlight the areas of your credibility, the accomplishments you've achieved throughout your life, the branding by association you have. Is this beginning to make sense...?! Go to the back page of this chapter and start making some notes.

What is your credibility? When people go to my website they see me with Sir Richard Branson, they read a very strategic biography, and they see that they can buy a copy of my bestselling book. Next, they see me being inducted into the International Investors Hall of Fame by Robert Kiyosaki someone who is highly credible, they look at all the pictures that are more branding by association, they look at the interviews I've done with highly credible individuals, and they look at the testimonials. This is a very strategically built website; I make hundreds of thousands of dollars every single year, off my credibility alone. I feel like tapping on your foreheads right now followed by the words "Hello McFly are you getting this?!"

Where are you placed right now? If you were to stand in front of me right now and you told me your name and I Google it, where and how would you show? Some people are not very strategic when it comes to social media. There are a bunch of photographs on places like Facebook and Twitter or Instagram of people looking like absolute idiots, and I am just being honest about it, not harsh. When you are Googled and these images turn up and you are there passed out from having a few too many drinks, maybe lying on grass, is that a strategic image that you want people to see?

Is that going to help your credibility, help your business, or is it going to impede you? Of course, the answer is it is going to impede, it's going to make it difficult for you. You have got to be more strategic in what you put out there in the world and especially in these days of the internet. *If I can Google you, I only want to see the best, most strategic information about you that is benefit-driven*, to help others make the decision to want to buy from you. Understand that all of this is done to help them make the decision to buy from you over the next person. Are you strategically thinking about this properly or not?

As I have said before, most people are invisible; if you are not on Google, you're no one. No matter who you think you may be, no matter what you may have accomplished in your life, if you are not on Google, you're a no one - you're invisible, it's as simple as that and quite honestly I'm here to kind of be in your face a little about it, because it's that important. You are making your life so much more difficult than it needs to be, should be, or could be. If you are highly credible and you have accomplishments that are good accomplishments in your industry, that can be beneficial to help people make the decision to want to buy from you over anyone else, *you must* showcase those and showcase them correctly and strategically.

Think of it like an online billboard, the billboards that we see down the streets that are advertising all the time; your online profile is your online billboard. What message do you want to get across to people? Make sure that you highlight it correctly, in a way that is only beneficial to you, you only highlight the benefits, and when I say "benefits" what I mean is the benefits that you bring to other peoples lives'.

In the early days, I was very worried about the fact that I lost the majority of my real estate through my divorce. Now I see that only as a positive, because now I can help other individuals to not make the same mistakes I made and I wouldn't have known what those mistakes were had I not gone through them myself. Sometimes what potentially you may believe as a negative, a gut wrenching negative, to some people can possibly be a huge positive, because now you are human, not a machine that just goes out and wins all the time. The people that have won the most have messed up the most, and it is really important you understand that. Don't be scared about messing up because if you are scared, guess what is going to happen? You are going to do exactly that - it is just the way it is, it's the law of attraction.

Be excited about what is going to happen, how you are going to impact others, and how it is going to make your life better and how when your life is better you can make other people's lives better; your partners, your family's. Be excited about that, don't get hung up on the negative side, leave that to everyone else because that's what they do best. Embrace the positivity that is going to come from making this huge change in your life. Make sure that your message says what you want it to say on your online billboard; it must say exactly what you want it to say - it must be strategic. Make sure that your biography is short sharp and to the point. You don't need fluff; don't care about fluff because you don't have much time to capture people's attention. You only have seconds to capture people's attention, so make sure it's strategically worded, short and to the point.

Do you know one of the coolest things about all of this, is that if you change your industry, if you are working one minute as a mortgage broker and then the next minute you are going selling cars, you can change the content of your website at the drop of a hat. You can write a new book that is in alignment with what you now do, this is where this is so powerful. We have seen people that go from one job to the next to the next, to the next, and quite honestly they become pretty unsuccessful in the majority of it because they are just guessing all the time; yet these are not strategic moves.

Anytime you make a shift in your industry; it may be a totally radical shift to a whole brand new industry, it may not. It may just be a slightly more niche area of the market; all of your content can be changed on your website on that same day. A new book can be written and in your hand in a very short period of time - this is very simple stuff. Are you starting to see and to recognize the importance of what I am talking about here?

The compounding of all of this information is radically important and has a direct link to your success. Every single time you accomplish something new, or you have a new image to put up; you can add it immediately - you don't have to sit there and hope people are going to see it – no, you just change it on your website immediately.

If, you get inducted into a Hall of Fame or something else highly credible, you can add that to your existing online billboard to compound again on the credibility you currently have. Again, we spoke about the importance of making sure your brand/logo is on your website; make sure that the images you put on your website are strategic images, no images of 'things' that is not going to show you as the authority in that industry.

What is the persona you want people to see about you? Create an online billboard around the persona you want people to see, the content you have, the area that you are the smartest person at. Make sure that your images rank high on Google, so that when people Google your name; not only is your name at the top of page one, but that when they click on your images they also all rank in Google - that they are shown.

Notes:

Google yourself right now and see exactly what shows, are you impressed with the results?

What images would show up?

What does your business card say on it?

What message do you want people to read about you?

Where is your credibility positioned?

What message do you want to get across to people?

If you move to a different industry or business what do you now do?

CHAPTER 8:

THE IMPORTANCE OF BECOMING A SPEAKER

If you are a speaker, there is no question that you are an authoritative figure within your industry. Why? If you have ever been to a seminar that's within your industry, or another industry, you have most likely seen speakers on stage, and some of them have said things that made an impact on you. You will have taken this information from them as highly credible information. Why? Because content they said actually made sense to you, you connected with them and their message. You view them as the authority because *they* are the ones on the stage, not you. Does this make sense? It's really important you understand the power of this.

When I first stood on stage, I prepared my content for many years, even though I was doing it subconsciously - on autopilot. But, when I stood on stage, I had thousands of people looking at me, and I asked myself "Why do these people want to listen to what I have to say?" Thankfully, I have done this long enough now to know these people listen to what I have to say because it is has impact – because it makes a positive difference in their lives and because everything I say is easy to do!

There is nothing similar to that feeling; it is the most empowering and humbling feeling in the world when you have all of these people listening to you. Why did they listen to me? Because I am a bestselling author and because I am highly credible online, so when I stand in front of a group of people no matter how small a group, usually they will have researched who the speaker is. They sit there and listen to what I have to say because of the credibility I already possess, the credibility that I have personally highlighted *strategically*. Otherwise, I would be just like anybody else, but I'm not. I looked at my life differently; I looked at what needed to be done, so people would take me seriously, because I knew that my message was impactful. I knew I could make a difference in people's lives and in their business. I'll tell you right now, when you make a positive impact in someone's business, you change their lives - it is as simple as that.

It is a very humbling experience, but you have to make sure you do become a speaker, because when you listen to a speaker, they are only speaking for one reason; they know what they are talking about and you have something to learn from them. They are the authority. I have already said that you cannot be in an industry for a number of years and not possess a large amount of in-depth information - information that can make and help other people's lives better.

How do you find the content for your speaking events? Here is the secret: all of the content you're going to need in the early stages of this comes from your book. Once you create the book, you've got content for your website and for your speaking engagements. You will also find, as time goes by that your content just grows - it evolves naturally, because you continue to learn new things. When I wrote my first book it was about customer service; now the content has evolved so much that I could write a volume of books. At some point a volume of books will be written. Here's number 2!

People listen to what I have to say because what I say is real and it makes an actual difference. People ask me "Don't you often get worried or nervous before you go up on stage?" My answer is always the same "A little maybe, just before I walk up I am a little bit nervous, because these people don't know who I am." I have spoken in front of enough people from around the world now to know that what I say makes a difference. I am no different to you, but we are probably just in different industries. The knowledge you possess, can make a difference to others and there is no other feeling in the world like the one where someone comes up and shakes your hand after being on stage and wants you to sign a copy of your book or wants their photo taken with you. When this first started happened to me I was really unprepared for what was going to happen next. Essentially, you became a rockstar for a really short period of time, and then you get addicted to it and you want more. When you see the people you're helping because of the content you're able to give, people just want more.

I accept that there are some speakers that are better than others; I class myself as a fantastic content speaker. What do I mean by that? I mean that I give great content away. I may not be the best person in the world in selling from stage - I find it a little bit uncomfortable if the truth be known. If you want to buy anything of mine, then buy it, and do so because you think it is going to be good and not because I am going to try and force you to buy it. However let me tell you something right now, if at any point I ever actually go to sell you anything it is because I honestly know you need it not because I want to sell you 'crap', I can't stand it when other speakers used to do that to me so I will not do it to you.

So, what advice can I give you on becoming a great speaker? It is so simple- just be yourself; the person that you are every day - be that person on stage. If you've seen me on stage, you know that I am a total goofball, you know that my language is maybe not the best and you have read it in this book, why? Because it is real - it is me. I accept that I do tone my language down when I am on stage.

However, I also gauge the audience and sometimes I push it on purpose.

I feel the energy from the audience and if I feel they want more from me and that I maybe need to have a bit more shock-value - shock and awe and all with my language, then I will do it - I drop the F bomb. I don't have a problem with it. Some people get offended by it and that is okay because it is impossible to satisfy everyone; it is the greater good for the greater number of people, and if the greater number of people understand it, get it, acknowledge it and it makes a positive impact on their life, then that is all I care about. I cannot and will not ever be able to keep everybody happy. For me, someone who is always a giver, it still frustrates me because I do want to make everybody happy and give, but the truth of the matter is that it is not always going to be that way.

So with that being said if you are a bit of a goofball and you like to tell jokes, then this is how you need to be on stage; just be you but a professional version of you. I have coached a lot of individuals to become speakers and I say the same thing time after time after time, be you. If you are not the type of person that is going to talk monotone to your family and friends, then don't stand up on stage and talk in a monotone voice. If you are someone that is very charismatic, then make sure that that comes across on stage, why? Because people get sucked in on it, they love it, they thrive on it, and they want more and more and more. I have had people that did not want me to get off stage because I am charismatic on stage; I am goofy, I am talking and telling jokes and laughing at myself all the time, or laughing at people in the audience all the time, but I never do anything that makes anybody feel uncomfortable and by the end of it we're all mates!

At the same time, I also take what I do very seriously, and if I find anyone in the audience that is not paying attention or paying respect for the rest of the room I have them removed from the room, why? Because it is the greater good for the greater number of people, and if one individual is affecting the group they will be removed - I have had it done before. I accept that not everybody wants to listen to what I have to say and that's okay. I don't have a problem with that, but I do have a problem if one person is affecting the experience for everyone else; that I do have a problem with absolutely.

It is vitally important to become a speaker, why? It's very simple, and this is the whole book right here for you: *when you are an author and you have strong online presence and you are an authoritative speaker within your industry, your credibility is so high that everybody and anybody wants to deal with you.*

They want to become your friend, they want to take you out, they want to siphon your brain, and they want your knowledge too, why? Because you possess what they want. Your credibility is everything - perception is everything; if you are perceived to be an idiot, then in their eyes you are an idiot, immaterial of whatever accomplishments you may have. If they Google you and find photos of you passed out with drinks all around you, their perception is that you are a drunk – it's as simple as that.

Perception is reality, so it is important to make sure that when you create your credibility you create it in alignment with who you are, what you do, and the fact that it is all about them and not you. I created this information for you. I don't have to do this; I didn't have to write the book. I wrote the book to make your life easier. When people make a big accomplishment in their lives they usually let me know, and when they let me know, they make me feel so far beyond awesome, I can't put into words that everything I do is for that feeling.

When you start to speak, make sure you take as many photos as possible of you on stage. If you are speaking before lunch, after lunch change your clothes, why? Because then you get two different photographs you can use. So, if you are speaking in the morning and you are wearing a white shirt, then after lunch change it to a blue, black or green shirt. This way you have two different photos that you can use in the early stages of your speaking career to give you some credibility. The more you speak, the more photos you take, and the more photos you take, the more credible you are, because you are now seen to be speaking everywhere. I know… Genius!

When I first started speaking, I had photos taken of me all over the place as many times as I could because I knew I needed people to see that I was a speaker. It was important for people to know that I was a speaker because the speaking side of it is really where my true passion lays. I could stand in front of thousands of people for hours and give to them and give to them - and give to them - because it fulfilled me. So, make sure that you utilize those photos; where are you going to utilize them? On your online billboard. They research you, they see you are an author, they have a look on your website and see that you have been speaking – is this all starting to make sense now?

Although you may find that speaking isn't something you are naturally good at or even want to do, but when you practice it over and over again you will be able to stand in front of people and know your stuff. When you know your stuff that is okay, and just before the very first words come out of your mouth… relax. Once you say the very first word you will relax, I want you to be aware of this. You know the content, this is not stuff that you have to learn, you are speaking about an area that you are already highly knowledgeable in.

Let me give you a great tip; when you have been in a seminar and you see the speaker talk, they have a slide show a PowerPoint presentation. My PowerPoint presentations are very simple - they are always bullet points. What the audience fails to realize is those bullet points are written for me as well as for them. Why do I say that?

When I created the presentation I did it with a beginning, middle and end with the fact that I needed to get out a certain amount of content. Every time I click on a screen, that bullet point reminds me of what I am going to talk about. The way I do it is this: if I have one screen with five bullet points, I start on bullet point one, then I talk about everything I can think of within reason relating to that bullet point. Once I finish that, what do you think I do? Very simple, I move to bullet point two and I do the exact same thing. Then I talk about bullet point three, bullet point four, bullet point five, and so on. So, the bullet points during the seminars are really for the speaker to make sure that he or she stays on track.

When I first starting speaking, there was no way I could stand up on stage for two days solid and remember every single thing I want to talk about. You may have seen people before that just step up and have little cards to remind them of what to say. Well, my cards are my PowerPoint presentation.

Once you practice enough times in your house, it is not difficult to do it in front of a bunch of other people, because you don't necessarily have to be looking at them all of the time. Quite honestly, it's much easier doing it in front of a bunch of people you don't know rather than people you know. However I do strongly suggest that you look every person in the audience and in the eyes at some point, this way you can really connect with them throughout the presentation, why? Because you want to build a rapport with them, let them know that you understand what they are going through.

For myself, I want to build a relationship with my audience, but when I'm done talking about one bullet point I look at my computer screen and look at the next bullet point. I get reminded about the point and talk about it, and then, guess what? I just move on and talk about it in very simple terms. Make sure you keep your talks simple but informative. I try not to get into too much complex complicated stuff; keep it simple all the time, find the easy way of explaining it.

I always like to give real gutsy information - real meat on the bone information. Like I said, I am an amazing content speaker; you want to know it, I'll cover it, and I will explain it in such a simple way that anybody and everybody can understand and I won't move on until I know that everybody does understand it. I don't want to walk off stage with people not understanding what I am talking about; otherwise I have not done my job correctly. So I always say, and you have heard me say in this book: "Does that make sense?" If it doesn't, I want people to tell me because I know I have another way of explaining so they *can* understand it, plus I've studied body language for many years so even if they lie to me and tell me that they do understand me and I see that their body says otherwise I will go over it again - does that make sense?

Make sure you give a lot of information; there is an old school of thinking which is: keep your best 'bits' to yourself, keep your secrets to yourself, and don't tell anybody else because they are your secrets. I come from a different school of thinking which is: "Tell them your secrets, tell them the things you know." Why? Because if you tell them something that is about to change their lives; a secret that maybe has taken you millions of dollars to figure out, a thousand dollars, years to figure out, and you give it to them for free, they will love you forever. They will continue to buy from you, they will continue to follow you and support you because they know that every time they get something from you, you will not hold back on them; you will give them the best parts.

You know, I am lucky that I get to coach people from all over the world in many different industries. The reason I can do this is because it is about the information you possess. I can sit there with you and pull out of you the information you will need so you can write your book, so you can create your website, so you can have the content you need to be speaking in front of all these people - it is very simple once you know how.

So, when you create your slideshow; the way I do it is very simple - what do I want to talk about? Well, I want to talk about creating credibility - what is that? I get a sheet of paper and write: creating credibility is about this, and it is about this and it is about this; I start to write down bullet points. By the end of it, after I have done it all, the presentation is complete. I just put it into PowerPoint or really Keynote and my presentation is done. I don't need to practice it too much at that point because the content I know is already in my head - I don't have to learn it, I just have to be reminded of what to say next. This is very simple and easy to use.

Also make sure that your brand and logo are on all of your slides; you want to make sure all of it is tied together properly. Hopefully you have gone to the notes section and made as many notes as you possibly can regarding being a speaker.

Remember, when you are creating content for your speaking, it is all about the audience - no one else matters. What information can you give to these people right here right now, that can change their lives forever - then present it in your style. Keep it light-hearted, keep it fun, keep it giggly, and keep it real and most importantly keep it informative.

Notes:

Have you ever considered becoming a speaker or the massive impact it has on your career?

What do you need to do for people to finally take you seriously?

How much content do you already possess inside of you to become a speaker today?

Where does the content for becoming a speaker come from?

How do you overcome nerves to become a speaker?

What is my advice to you about becoming a great speaker?

Why should you take photos when you are on stage and how many?

CHAPTER 9:

CONNECTING IT ALL TOGETHER

As I have mentioned in previous chapters, it is so important to make sure that everything you are creating here for your credibility, is for the direction you want your life to go – the direction of your career. You may be taking a change of direction from your industry - you may be going from one industry to another - you may be a business owner who wants to increase your own credibility so that your business can become more successful and profitable. You may be starting off fresh - you may be fresh out of school or fresh out of education and want to start a new business. You may be sick to death of the industry you're currently in and want to change; the important thing is that every single thing you create needs to have a direct link - a direct connection to exactly what it is you do in your career.

If you are a baker, then your website wants to be created around the previous accomplishments you had as a baker, the successful years you've been doing it and what makes you different from any other baker out there, meaning awards, publicity, promotion, leverage etc. If you're a baker and you write a book, your book wants to be about how to make the perfect loaf of bread or how to make the perfect pastry or the perfect loaf of bread in five steps or five minutes or five things you need to know about making the perfect loaf of bread in under five minutes. Whatever it is, whatever industry it is that you're in; the book must be 100% in alignment with your industry as must be the content on your website and the same with the content for your speaking.

As I said in previous chapters, you can tweak your website content as time goes by. When I started my website, all I had on my first piece of credibility was the fact that in 2009 I was inducted into the International Investor's Hall of Fame, which ok granted is a pretty big one, although I didn't see it as that at the time. Since then I have been able to add all the images of me with my highly credible friends - entrepreneurs, celebrities, and so on. I have been able to add my book and now this one will get added, I have added my speaking engagements, added the fact that I can and have helped people become financially free through my knowledge and mentorship within real estate. I have helped people become more successful in their relationships, in their marriage and in their businesses, why? Because I get it, I understand it. I have studied master business practices and human psychology and behaviour from the worlds greatest my entire life (I literally mean my entire life) and I have worked and coached enough people to know and recognize the patterns. Once I recognize their patterns then I know how to fix it every single time, both patterns of success and patterns of failure - very simple.

All of your content must and needs to be 100% in alignment with what you do. If you were a baker or you create credibility based around being a baker and baking the perfect loaf of bread, and all of a sudden you decide that two to three years down the road you have had enough of baking and now you've saved money and want to be a real estate investor. You write your book on real estate, you change the content on your website and change the content for your speaking engagements and you explain why and how you made the transition - and like I said before - the majority of the content that you need really will come from your book. When I stand on stage in front of large groups of people at seminars and I speak about creating credibility, there is content I can pull from my book and there are additional things I add to it as and when more information comes to me, to help make the process easier and simpler for my customers… you! I cannot over emphasize this enough just how important it is that you must connect every single thing together, to relate it to the industry you're in - it is *so* important.

Do not write a book on baking bread if you are a real estate investor. Do not write a book on real estate if you sell websites, I'm trying to give you diverse examples. Your book must absolutely 100% be in alignment with what you do at that moment; it can be changed should you choose to take a redirection in your life - in what you do for a living. Make sure that every time you present your information, whether it is on the internet, or through the book, or speaking, make sure you keep it clean and simple. When I say clean - don't complicate the process.

People love to use big words all the time, avoid that if you can, keep it simple all the time. Don't over complicate a process that doesn't need to be complicated - there is only one person that matters and that's the customer. So, let's make it as simple as possible for them to understand what we want to tell them.

When I am on stage, people are captivated by what I say, because I keep it easy and simple. I'm not out to make myself look like I am awesome, or that I am all this and all that like some other speakers do, because I am not - I am Just Ian Houghton, who happens to possess an area of knowledge that does make a massive difference to millions of people's lives once they know it.... your life. Make sure your book is very industry specific; don't write a book on dogs if you are in real estate or don't write a book on dogs if you make dancing shoes. I say dancing shoes because I had a student that made dancing shoes. So, what did I say to the student who made dancing shoes? Write a book about the perfect dancing shoes, and he said "What do you mean?"

The thing is, when someone has done something for such a long time they possess a depth of information, but the problem is, they don't realize that. So, when I am talking to him, I said "Well, why do you make those dancing shoes the way you make them?" He said "Well, because I found out that if I use this type of leather it has this type of effect and they last longer and look better, and so on." Now, the truth of the matter is, he knows this because he has done it for years and he possesses knowledge that not even he is aware of - I didn't have that knowledge, but it needs to be highlighted by him. Why do you cut the leather on the dancing shoes in a certain way? Why do you have them stitched this way? What type of stitching do you use and why? What measurements do you take and why do you take them, and are they important? And, if they are important, why are they important?

You see there just so much you can talk about. Granted this may be of no use to you at all but let me tell you something. If you are a dancer and you are just about to buy a new pair of dancing shoes and you saw this book how likely are you to not only buy it but actually read it? Highly highly likely! Then let me ask you my next question, how many of his clients are at that stage? Every single one of them!

Sometimes we just need to get back to the basics; help customers understand a subject from the basic point of view first and then we can crank them up and get into a little bit more gutsy information the 'meet on the bone' information, but one of the things I will never do is over complicate a process. I will always make it simpler, and then if I need to, then I can really go deeper into it. Other than that, keep it easy, keep it simple, and make sure that it is understandable by anyone who picks up the book - from a nine year old to a ninety year old. The easier you keep the process the more of a connection you will have with the customer.

Notes:

If you write a book or build a website or become a speaker, what should your content be about?

Why should we tweak our website?

When should we tweak our website?

What do we add to our website?

How important is it to connect everything together and why?

CHAPTER 10:

TWEAKING THE FOUNDATIONAL WORK

Creating credibility is what I call the foundational work. I have already explained in multiple chapters the importance of being able to tweak the content we create as and when we need to. Either if we need to amend it by adding to it, or we take a total redirection of our careers in our lives. The important thing to understand is that your foundational work is complete. I have said this before; you can change the content on your website by adding to it or totally rehashing it. You can also write a whole new book, and from the book can also come all new content for your speaking engagements. This is so important to understand, because when you are moving forward in your life, the content always evolves. The website that I have now will not look the same in twelve months, and it certainly won't look the same in five, ten, fifteen or twenty years. Why? Because I am always actively, consciously amending it, changing it, and doing new things in my life, but the truth of the matter is, the foundational work of it is now done and it is done forever, I am now a highly credible individual. Once it is complete it's done and it really doesn't take long to get that information complete. It is all about one thing and one thing only: JFDI - Just F***ing Do It!

You will see as you progress and start to create your own credibility now from the information in this book how easy it is to change the foundational work when you need to. We have put the foundation for your 'house' in and we have built your career, which is the house on that foundation. If you want to change you house - change your career - we just build it on top of the foundation that already exists why, because it's solid.

The simple fact that you've build it from the early stages, means that it's going to be strong; that foundation is always going to be there. Write a new book if you need to, but it is so important to understand that I look at my website all the time and I amend it frequently. Anytime something new has happened, I put it on there; I leverage the fact that I am becoming more and more credible all the time, and then I leverage that into further business opportunities. There is a real science to this, real technology involved in making this stuff happen, and once you get it, once you understand it, you can do anything you want to achieve in life.

Now you can do it as someone that is credible - you are not invisible anymore, you are not a no one - you are now a someone; the type of someone that everybody else shuts up when you walk into the room, and they want to listen to you speak, because they know, that you know what you're talking about and they want to learn from you.

This is not the Ian Houghton show, I don't care about me, I care about you, I want to give you some examples of how this has impacted my life. I was at a big event with a very well known celebrity friend of mine. I walked into the event and it was full of other very well known celebrities. My friend was asked who I was, by the other celebrities, and he explained who I was. Immediately, I had credibility because I was with him as his guest and he positioned me when they asked who I was. So, they asked me questions about what I did, why I was with this person, and so on and so forth. Within a very short space of time, about ten to fifteen minutes, I had control of that room. Why? Because I knew my content, I knew my stuff, I knew that I was impactful, and I knew that what I had to say would make a difference for those people because probably no one had the guts to say it to them before.

It doesn't matter how much money some people may or may not have, or how much credibility some people may or may not have, how much of a celebrity they are, or how well-known they are. I know that the information I possess can and does make a massive difference in anyone and everybody's life, and that is why I can walk into a room and have total confidence within myself and my knowledge; because I know my content is powerful and makes a real profound difference. I'm confident in myself, my abilities and my content. What do I mean when I say I take control?

Everybody wants to talk to you, people crowd around you, everybody wants to know the information you know, so they can have a better life, so you can make their journey easier and less painful. It doesn't matter how successful people are in the world, most want more and better in life. If someone is put in front of us who can provide information for a happier and better, more fulfilled life - you better believe they shut up and pay attention to what that person has to say. I don't believe I am better than anybody else; I just possess a deep level of knowledge that makes an incredible impact on people and their lives for the positive. My foundational work is done, but it is always being tweaked.

All of this stuff I have spoken about in this book is so simple; I know you know this, it is in your hands now. I have given you all the information that I can. The foundational work, once complete, is always complete.

Notes:

What is the 'Foundational work'?

Why is it important to tweak the foundational work?

How can you now leverage this foundational work?

Can you leverage all the foundational work into future business and if so where?

Are you prepared for all the opportunities heading your way?

How can you better prepare yourself?

CHAPTER 11:

COACHES AND MENTORS

I never realized the massive importance of coaches and mentors in my life and in my journey. You know, I've always been someone that has kind of fought hard in my life, figuring out ways to make this happen and make that happen, and people that know me know that I was pretty useless at school and I left school at the age of 16. I just wasn't academic.

It wasn't the way I needed or wanted to learn. When I was in school, I knew that the information they were teaching me was going to be 100% irrelevant to me in my life. Of all the stuff I learned in school, I knew that there were truly only two subjects that were really the important, which were math and English. There

I was, wasting my time in school, sitting there, learning about stuff that I didn't even care about. Then being told that calculators and reference books and all that were not available to me in the middle of exams, when I would scratch my head and say, "Well, why? Are they not available to us in real life?" It just wasn't for me.

So, I always had a massive problem with the academic education system and the moment I had an opportunity to leave, I ran, because it just wasn't my form of education. My father told me, as I got older, "Ian, the teacher will be found when the student is ready to be taught." Which is a very well-known saying and it was really important because what hit me was this: As I got older and as I started to hit a big failure through my divorce, I realized that I really needed to gain knowledge. Let me tell you something that I've learned on my journey.

Every single time something goes wrong, it is the world, it is the universe, highlighting to you that you are under-knowledged in that specific area. Whatever has just gone wrong, it means that you are under-knowledged in that specific area. Therefore, what I've learned in life now, is that we can go and find out where we have made a mistake, we can utilize the internet to become highly knowledgeable on that subject, whatever it is, and we can make sure that mistake never happens again, once we possess the relevant knowledge.

On the other side of things, if information is not available to us, one of the things I have done now as I've gotten older, and this has massively reduced my learning curve and made my journey a lot easier, is I've put my hand in my pocket and I've paid thousands of dollars, tens of thousands, *hundreds* of thousands of dollars to be coached and mentored by someone that can get me the information I need to get me to the next level. Does that make sense? It's so funny, right? Because when I first moved to America, all I saw and heard were Americans talking about, "I'm going to go to this college!" Or, "I've got this degree or this qualification and I've spent all these years learning this stuff and I've got, all of this student debt, but, you know, I've now got a really great paying job."

I call those people 'highly educated, high-taxpayers.' I never wanted to be that way. I never wanted that to be how I viewed things, but I knew that if I were to go and get a coach or mentor that they could make my life significantly easier. Now I go to different people for different things. So, if I know I need to learn how to write the best sales copy or whatever it may be, I find the best in the world pay for their knowledge and I learn from them. Most people don't do that. Most people don't do that to begin with and then if they do go to learn from someone, they go to learn from someone that's maybe *just good enough* rather than the best of the best. I'm only ever, ever interested in learning the best information or the world's greatest information from the world's greatest individuals, because I don't want to waste my time.

I need to go to the best of the best so I can be the best of the best. Does this all make sense to you? It's so funny because when you look at these people that have spent so much of their time and their money to really only become highly educated, high-taxpayers and yet they won't stick their hand in their pocket for $10,000 or $20,000 or even $1,000 or $1,500 or whatever it may be, just to get the knowledge they need to get there and help them overcome the obstacle or hurdle before them. Yet, if you can change your viewpoint and look at it and say, "Look, I need to go to this person; I need to go to Ian to help me create my credibility." Or, "I need to go to this person to help me gain some knowledge in something that I'm not knowledgeable in." JDFI. Don't waste any time. Stop holding yourself back.

There is one thing we don't have much of and realistically that is time. We don't know when our lives are over, so we have to keep moving forward all the time. You need to reduce the amount of time it takes you to do things and make mistakes.

Let me tell you something else about coaches and mentors. When I was in my 20's, I thought, "I'm going to go out there and do it and make it happen, and I'll figure it out along the way."

It was just mistake, mistake, mistake, mistake, *mistake*! But, as I got older, my thought process changed and now, I want to reduce the mistakes so I am going to go find out who's the best of the best, learn from them, then I'll go and do it. Now I don't make mistakes! Simple.

It's such simplistic thinking, yet so many people don't do it because they think they have to go out there and make the mistakes. You don't! Success leaves clues. Follow and study successful people or pay for their time to teach you and you'll reduce your learning curve. You don't have a problem in spending $75,000 to $100,000 to be a doctor or whatever degree you have, but you struggle sticking your hand in your pocket for $1,000 or $1,500 or $20,000 or $50,000 to help you get to where you really want to be. I always scratch my head on that one. It's not the smartest thinking in the world because all you are doing is making your job and your journey longer, more difficult, way more expensive and way more painful than it actually needs to be.

Now, I want to tell you something that hit me. It was right after I was inducted into the International Investors Hall of Fame. What hit me was this: I realized that there was some really amazing, incredibly powerful, high-end information out there. Now, this high-end information isn't cheap. It's actually bloody expensive. But, whatever you spend on this high-end information that is available to you out there, and as long as you action it, that's the whole point of JFDI, as long as you "Just F***ing Do It", you won't have a problem. Now, like I said, this stuff isn't cheap and it comes at a premium, but the reason it comes at a premium is because it bloody works. However, it only works if you do it. If you read or follow the information and don't do it, then guess what type of results you're going to get. Just think about that for a second... None. Right? You have to JFDI!

We can get the information very, very quickly and there is an abundance of high-end powerful information, out there. For whatever it is that you're wanting, whether it be real estate; investments; personal development or personal transformation, moving you to the next level, personal branding whatever it may be; whether it's about business; a specific area of business such as sales, marketing; whether it's a specific industry, it doesn't matter. The point is that high-end information exists out there.

Yes, it comes at a premium. However, if you get the information and you study it until it sticks and becomes part of you, you'll have no problem. That money you've spent and the money I've spent in my education through my coaches and mentors, I'd spend it again and again, and again, because I wouldn't be who I am or where I am today if I hadn't done it. So, it's really important that you do not become a penny pincher when you think about your personal growth and journey in your life. Sometimes we have to stick our hand in our pocket, but by doing that, it moves us to the next level, in fact it explodes us to the next level.

I realize as I'm sitting here and I'm writing this book that I've actually spent *over* a jaw-dropping, $5 million dollars on my education; $5 million in successes, in failures, in studying, in seminars, in paying for people's time, in paying for products, in paying for programs. Basically, I've paid for the information that I need so I stop messing up and make the journey as easy as possible for me. Again, I of all people know it's not cheap, but what I can tell you is this: I spent $15,000 on my education for real estate. I walked out 3 days later with the information and knowledge that 3 months after that allowed me to close on a $2 million piece of real estate, and just by closing on that deal, allowed me to financially retire. Now that's money well spent!

So, let me ask you a question. Would you spend $15,000 right now to know that $15,000 was going to retire you financially that you never had to worry about money again? I think that's pretty obvious, right? That's a no-brainer. Of course you would. So, it's important that you don't become penny pinchers at this. Sometimes, we all have to pay for high-end information. That's one of the reasons my hourly fee has exploded, and as I continue to develop my depth of content I continue to grow too, because I can make a deeper, more impactful impression on people's lives. That is why your time becomes so valuable.

You know, you're reading this right now and you possess an area of knowledge that I don't. And then, maybe, I may come to you and pay you your fee, for that information. I may say, "I just need to get the information from you now" and you may give that to me and it might cost me whatever it costs me but if you reduce my learning curve and stop me from messing up I'll be happy to pay it.

As time goes by my hourly fee is slowly creeping up. There's a very good chance that by the time this book comes out and by the time the volume of people who want my help and advice to make their journey easier have gone up that my hourly fee has gone up even more. It has to. When you become more and more in demand, you have to look at your time and ask how valuable it is to you. I'll tell you straight out, my 'personal time', my time that I'm not with clients my time at night or the weekends is, hands down, way more valuable than my 'working time'. What do I mean by that? If you want me, as I write this book right now, my hourly fee is a certain amount in my 'working time'. Now, if you want my time when I'm sitting on my sofa, watching the TV or buried in my phone creating content for my next new book or product so I can help your journey, and you want that time, that is my *personal* time.

I value my personal time at least double my 'work time' rate.

Why? Well that's my creative time. That's my time for growth. That's my time for learning, for becoming better, for building a stronger muscle in business, in finances, in investments, in financial freedom, in having more fun. People that know me personally know I'm all about the fun 24 hours a day, 7 days a week. I'm Party-Guy. It has nothing to do with alcohol or anything like that. It's just the personality I have. However, when I'm on my own, and someone wants my time, my personal time, you have to be prepared to pay a lot of money for that because that is very, very valuable time for me.

Now, when I'm in the set hours of normal work hours of 9 to 5, if I choose to work 9 to 5, if I even choose to work at all, then, okay, I'm at my normal hourly rate. But, you want me out of that time? I'm more than that because my private time is very, very, very valuable to me.

What's also so amazing is that I learned that there is an incredible amount of high-end information out there. That if we just humble ourselves and keep our mouths shut and listen and learn, we can become so unbelievably knowledgeable in such a short space of time. Let me tell you something. When I want to learn something, I throw myself into it, literally from the moment I wake up until the moment I pass out. I usually have my head buried in it for a couple of weeks, 2, 3, maybe 4 weeks. But, I'll tell you what, by the time I've come out of it, there are not many people that are as knowledgeable in that subject as I am.

The truth of the matter is that we only have to really throw ourselves into it for a couple of weeks, literally from the moment you wake up until the moment you go to sleep, and you can become so incredibly knowledgeable in something, you won't believe the type of information you can take on in that short amount of time. I have had life changing moments in hours, not years or days or weeks or months, but hours because I'm now aware of who I need to go to for the information I need to get me to the next level. Sometimes I have to pay a lot of money for that, but it is what it is. However, whatever I've paid, I know I'm going to get 20x back, easily.

Like I said to you earlier on in this book, my advice is that when you choose a coach or a mentor, you choose someone that has had both successes and failures and back to success, okay? That's really important. First of all, we want someone that is successful because they know patterns of success. Then, we want someone that's failed because we want them to point out to us the patterns of failure. They recognize them; you don't if you've never failed. It's as simple as that. Okay? But, then you want to make sure that the person has succeeded again. You know, at the end of the day, things will either make us or break us, and my successes and, specifically, my failures 100% made me who I am today. There is no question about it. I wouldn't be the individual I am had I not really messed up earlier on in my life. It made me stronger! It's so important to realize that when you go and find a mentor, find someone that succeeded, failed, and re-succeeded and succeeded stronger and better, because they will 100% stop you from failing.

You know one of the reasons why? In fact, let me ask you a question. Would you pay me $20,000 for a day of my time, not even a day of my time, about three-quarters of a day of my time for me to show you and teach you how to never financially fail ever again? Do you think that's worth $20,000?

If you own real estate and let's say you own a million dollar's worth of real estate and you want a couple of days of my time. You pay me $50,000 for two days of my time and during that time, I show you how never to lose your real estate. How to never get sued, never lose your property through foreclosure or divorce. Do you think that's worth the money you paid me? Absolutely it is!

$50,000 to save a $1 million, it's a no brainer. So remember, don't be penny pinching.

Look at how you can humble yourself in areas where you are not knowledgeable and pay someone good money to fill in the gaps you have. One of the reasons I can teach you all of this, is because I've been through it already. I know the things you need to do and say, and in what order and to whom. That's why this is so important. Sometimes we just have to pay that money to get the knowledge we need to reduce our learning curve.

I'll tell you, every single time I've done it, it's paid me back more, way more than what it's cost me to acquire that knowledge and I've gotten there faster, quicker and, quite honestly, cheaper, significantly cheaper than if I'd 'tried to figure it out myself. These coaches and mentors can make your life and journey so much easier. You'll find that as you move up the ladder, you'll want more and more and more of this information, and the more you want, the more you get, the more you'll want to go after again. Then you'll realize that, 'hang on a minute, I'm willing to pay more and more money, because I know that they're making my journey easier for me'. Understand that whatever you pay, you're going to get it back 20x over, whether it be financially, emotionally, mentally, spiritually, whatever it is. There are people out there who possess this information that can make your journey easier. Don't waste your time. If you need my help or if you need to help someone else, reach out. But, be aware and be prepared to pay for it. JFDI!

If there's one thing I've done throughout my life and, specifically, over the past couple of years, I've stopped giving my information away for free. Here's why. I've learned this recently. There's a thing in business called a criminal exchange. A criminal exchange is when one thing goes one way, but nothing comes back the other way. What I realized was....If we give something for free, it immediately has zero value. What do I mean by that? Well, let me give you an example.

Imagine that there was a concert one evening. I know this is a random example, but go with it. Imagine that there is a concert taking place and you didn't buy tickets to it. A friend calls you up and says, "Hey, I've got tickets, I can't go, would you like my tickets for free?" You decide at that point, "Yes I do want the tickets, I'll go." Now, if it was a band that you were not all that interested about seeing, halfway through, you'll probably get up and walk out if it wasn't particularly brilliant. Why? Because the concert had zero value to you. You didn't pay for it. But, if you paid $20 or £20 or $200 or £200, you better believe that you will sit there and get your money's worth. So, the reason I don't give away information for free now is because people put no value on that type of information. You want my information, you have to pay for it. You may be saying, "Well, you're giving me this information now for free." No, I'm not. You've paid for the book. That's why you get this information. You get it because you paid for it and now there is no longer a criminal exchange. You paid me the money and I gave you my knowledge. It's as simple as that. Makes a lot of sense, right? So, no more giving information away for free!

I'm not saying that you keep everything close to your chest, but if someone says to you, "Oh, will you come and help me, will you coach me, will you mentor me for free?" The answer is no, I can't do it. I get a lot of people ask me, "Ian, will you coach me for free, as a way of giving back?" It's tough, and the main reason being, is the phrase I used previously… "If we give something for free, it immediately has zero value", also I'd love to coach you all for free, but, at the same time, I've got to get paid for the hard work and effort I've put into my education and I obviously need to claim that money back. This is why I did it. I did it for growth, but I also did it for my financial success and my financial future, too. Does this make sense? So, don't question anyone when you realize what they charge for their time and knowledge because what they give you will be more than what you've paid for, as long as you get out there and JFDI!

Notes:

Where do you believe you are under-knowledged?

Are you already paying good money for high-end information?

Are you currently held back in life due to a lack of knowledge in a specific area of life?

Are you reducing your learning curve by getting the best of the best information from the best of the best people?

How much time does it take to become highly knowledgeable within something?

Why is it important to find a coach or mentor that has both succeeded and failed and succeeded again?

Why do we not give our information away for free?

What does 'criminal exchange' mean, and why is it so important to you?

An Example

If you are a realtor and you want to be the top realtor here is how I would do it.

1. Write one book aimed at how to sell your home for your clients selling their home. Give all your secrets away and give them the book for free. (Do this on your first meeting with them)

2. Then write another book about how to buy your home at the correct price and again give all your secrets away and give your clients the book for free. (Do this on your first meeting with them). Now you have covered both sellers and buyers and you look like a rockstar to both of them. This will now get you more listings than any other agent and you will also get more sales too.

3. Write another book on how to be the best realtor, cover things such as looking after the customer, finding the customer. Basically teach all your stuff within your book so they can become more successful. Don't worry about giving them your best stuff they will still think you are better than them anyway.

4. Next create the content you're going to speak about. (This comes from your books)

5. Find an event that all the realtors in your area go to and contact them, tell them about your book(s) and ask for a chance to speak to them as a group.

6. Take your book on how to be the best realtor with you and

hand them to everyone.

7. Make sure that your website and online presence is strong and strategic.

That's it!

I guarantee you everyone will look at you radically different and none of what I have said is difficult at all. Not only that, but you will get a lot of business from it too. People will want to take you to lunch and they'll want a lot of free 'stuff' from you. That 'stuff' they want from you they will have to pay for it, make sure that you remember that.

CONCLUSION

We spoke in chapter one about the fact that most people are invisible; 99% of people are invisible, which is making their/your life more difficult - it is affecting you as you move forward in your career. The brand that you have right now needs to be based around you as an individual; it is about your brand - it is about Ian Houghton's brand, and the 'Jo Blogs' brand, not the brand of the business. We brand you first and then your business second, and we know now that so many people get this wrong. This is why we now know that successful people become more successful, because their brand is established, as is their credibility.

I explained about how my life was before I became credible; it was a lot more difficult in real estate because no one would take me seriously because I was a no one - I was unbranded and I was not credible. I explained about the fact that you may feel like you are already highly credible in your area right now, but my question to you is, are you credible locally, nationally or internationally? Most people at best are credible within their own town; if that, how credible do you want to be?

You discovered that for the first time you are able to get the exact message out that you want to put out, the question is what is the message you want to put out there? Whatever it may be, we now know that the technology is available to make that happen anytime, and we know that we can amend it any time we need to.

So many people have all of these qualifications from schools; degrees, Master's but they don't highlight them. We know that the technology is available, the information is available so we can highlight these qualifications strategically. You know that it is important to be highly credible, to make yourself credible in the eyes of other people, to make yourself highly visible!

You now know the importance to leveraging the existing knowledge you currently possess, and we know people don't take you seriously if you are not credible, even if *you* believe that you are credible. If it is not shown or highlighted strategically, people are going to find it difficult to take you as a credible individual.

You've learned that people are going to struggle to do business with you, no matter what industry you are in, if you are not highlighted as a credible person within your field, and we certainly

160

know that if you are not Googable you are 'no one' - you are invisible. We know that your brand needs to be created around you; no brand, no credibility, and you discovered that you can close deals purely off your credibility alone. People will deal with you; they will lend you money and want to get into business with you, if you are credible.

You can get the jobs you have always wanted to get, when you are credible. This is now a space for you to show off/highlight the skills that you have accomplished in your life. You can tell your stories and get them across in a way that highlights your credibility and everything you've accomplished in life.

We know that most people are already highly credible, they just don't know how to leverage it. I knew that I wasn't leveraging my own credibility until it was pointed out to me. The students I have worked with who weren't highly credible when they first started working with me, are now highly credible individuals because they took the information I gave them and utilized it, and have put it into their foundation work.

We spoke about the fact that most people are just unaware of what is going on around them, constantly living in a state of subconscious awareness - on autopilot. You put years of the information you have into accomplishing things, yet you don't highlight them in a way that makes you shine as a credible individual - that highlights the information you already possess. If you don't highlight it, you are like everyone else. It is about you separating yourself from everyone else and highlighting yourself strategically.

You possess a depth of knowledge that you gained throughout your life - you need to make sure it is highlighted and displayed in a highly strategic credible way. You discovered that most people don't think of the importance of thinking strategically or placing themselves strategically. We know that most people don't even know what being strategic really even means. The fact that when we are in front of individuals we don't think about ourselves strategically enough, we don't think about what we say as strategic, we don't think about what we do as strategic. We know that if we think and we act strategic in an area of life that we are passionate about that we will be the best at what we do, because we will always want to continue to educate ourselves in an area we are passionate in.... it's never work when it becomes our hobby.

When we educate ourselves in an area we are passionate in, we become the best at what we do. People will buy from you because you are passionate and highly knowledgeable plus it keeps you on top of your game within your industry - maintaining you as the authority within your industry. I knew that my abilities were great when I was younger, but the problem was that I wasn't thinking strategically and I wasn't highlighting it in a strategic format.

You now know the ways that are available to become highly credible by becoming an author and writing a book, having a strong online presence, and by becoming an authoritative speaker within your industry. You discovered the importance of branding yourself by association; leveraging other people's brands and creating your brand - what is your brand? Making sure that you have a logo that is specific to you as an individual and not your business, and tying every single thing together.

We know that we can leverage other people's brands. You now know to look within your friends; do you have highly credible friends, are you able to leverage their credibility? If not, do they have somebody that they can introduce you to that you could leverage their credibility? Start to gain knowledge from other people, start to brand by association off other individuals.

You know that you are going to ask people for introductions to other people. When they introduce you to them, you break down a barrier. You know that all of these things start to compound on each other and begin to make you highly credible. Being an author is highly credible; all of them together are very powerful and very highly credible.

We spoke about the importance of becoming an author, what it did for me and my life, taking me from a 'no one' to 'someone' literally overnight and how all of a sudden people looked at me differently and took me differently. They wanted to listen to me, they wanted to hear my story and learn from me - all because I wrote a book. Their perception of me had changed forever!

You know that your credibility in general becomes higher because you are an author. You can utilize your book as our business card because we want to get our information out there to the universe.

You discovered the importance of high online credibility and that the first thing people do nowadays is Google you. If you are not "Googable" you are a 'no one' it's as simple as that, you are invisible, which means you're making *your* life more difficult. It makes it more difficult for people who want to work with you, no matter how much you may have accomplished. You know it is up to you to position yourself correctly online- to be very strategic in what you say and how you say it!

You now have the knowledge you need to create an online billboard and to make sure that your message is in alignment with the direction that you want to go. You are going to use it to tell your stories and again to build on your brand utilizing your logo.

We spoke about the importance of you being a speaker and about how you being a speaker positions you as an authority in that specific field. People sit and listen to what you have to say because you are now a 'someone'. We spoke about how easy it is to create content for speaking purely from the content within your book, and how when you practice and practice - three, four, five hours a day for just one week – that's all you'll need to nail it!

Conclusion

It is important for you to just be yourself on stage – be able to laugh and, joke around, if that's who you are. If you were sitting in the audience, what would you want to see from the presenter - from the keynote speaker? Be that person; make it fun, make it enjoyable and easy for people to understand and don't bore the hell out of your audience.

You now know now that your presentation is set up based on a series of bullet points that keep you informed and keep you moving along in the direction you set up in the beginning. You want to make sure that you don't fail to tell anyone the information they need to be told, keeping your talk simple but highly informative. Also make sure that your brand and your logo are on your slides too.

You discovered the importance of making sure that you connect every single thing into the industry you are currently in. If we manufacture cars or houses then we don't write a book about how to make the perfect pancake. We write the book and we create our online presence in alignment with our current career, or the new career we are moving forward with - whatever that may be.

We learned that all of your logos including all of your branding needs to be on every single thing you do, and in all of your content, once your book is complete.

You now know that once your foundational work is complete, and your foundational work is to become an author, you want to

have a high and strong online presence and become a speaker within your industry. Once the foundational work is complete, all you need to do is tweak it at any point, amend it, update it - if there is a change in your career - you tweak all that information. You don't have to build a new website, the website is already built, and only the written words need change. The words in your book can change, or you can write a new book. Once you have the technology for writing a book, you can write another anytime you want, and once you have the book, you have the information you need to stand on stage.

We explained about the fact that I am always amending my information; changing the content on my website. The fact that when I speak, I am always tweaking it, always changing it, and doing something new. Does it work, does it not work? If it works, I do it again, and if it doesn't work, I don't do it again.

We spoke about how important my mentors have been through my life and how much I have learned from my mentors and coaches, and the importance of having a mentor and coach at the time you need them, which, quite honestly, is all the time. You need someone to hold you accountable.

People will spend years and tens of thousands of dollars to get another qualification that, quite honestly, has little impact on their life other than framing a piece of paper and putting it on a wall. Whereas you can be really smart and savvy and go to the best person in the world that has that information, pay them to teach you it, reduce your learning curve, and then immediately go out and implement it. This is what I do and why I keep growing and becoming stronger and stronger. We are not trying to reinvent the wheel, we are taking the right wheel and applying it to the right vehicle - that is all we are doing.

We know that there is an abundance of high-end information out there that you have to put your hand into your pocket and pay for. Now, when you do this we know it's not cheap, but we also know that the information we just paid for, if put into action, will change our lives. You also know that I have spent millions of dollars on my education and I know that by going to someone who already possesses the information I need massively reduces my learning curve and mistakes. It's the exact same for you!

You know that I view my personal time as so much more valuable than my 'work time'. This is where I can become highly creative. This is where I produce new products, write new books, discover new knowledge, grow in knowledge and become all around stronger, better etc.

We know that sometimes we need to keep our mouth shut and listen to what others have to say, listen and learn from what these other people can teach us to make life easier. Plus, we know that we only need a very short amount of time to learn this stuff, to become highly knowledgeable in it.

We know that when choosing a coach or mentor that you choose someone with both successes and failures in life. This way your coach or mentor can spot possible patterns of success and failure, and therefore massively reduce your risk of making a mistake.

We know that we do not give our information away for free because it has little to no value to the person that hears it. They must pay for your information for it to have any value to them. Once it has value then it has worth to them.

So… with all this being said, it has been an absolute pleasure for me to write this book for you and I cannot wait to hear the huge success stories coming from this one book alone. It has been my absolute pleasure to go through my life experiences (even though bloody tough at times) to write this for you to make your process, your journey easier. I look forward to shaking your hand, watching your success videos, reading the emails and letters you send me because I have taken the time to put my knowledge and information out for you, and I know you will appreciate it. You now need to realize, as much as you appreciate what I have done for you, your future customers will also appreciate what you do for them.

It is all about making a difference in this world, helping others succeed; it is the most humbling and exciting feeling you will ever experience in your life, and I am proud and privileged to be part of this small part of your journey.

Now, the book is over, there is just one thing left for you to do... JFDI!

Thank you!

www.CreatingCredibility.com

www.ingramcontent.com/pod-product-compliance
Lightning Source LLC
Chambersburg PA
CBHW050120210326
41519CB00015BA/4047